Walks for Families
in North Norfolk

Delia Malim

Walks for Families
in North Norfolk

Delia Malim

M A L I M   R O B I N S O N

Dedication

This book is dedicated to my mother and father with whom I first learnt to love Norfolk and to my daughters Martha and Constance who began, on these walks, to love it too.

Text © Delia Malim
Main cover photograph of Blakeney Harbour.
All photographs © Malim Robinson except p54 © Steve Wright.
Published by Malim Robinson, 2003. www.malimrobin.co.uk

ISBN 0 9544862 0 X

Printed and bound by Barnwells Print, Aylsham, Norfolk

Contents

The Walks

Acknowledgements

Much of my background information came from two invaluable sources: *The Norfolk Guide* by Wilhelmine Harrod and *The Companion Guide to East Anglia* by John Seymour. I am also grateful to the National Trust for their comprehensive guides to Sheringham and Felbrigg Parks and West Runton Heath, and to Lord and Lady Walpole for information on the Mannington Estate.

Thanks are owed to Robin Combes and the Bayfield Estate for permission to include a walk along the Glaven valley.

Finally, I must thank my husband David, for preparing the artwork for this book, for many of the photographs, including that on the cover, and not least for his company on the walks themselves.

Location of Walks

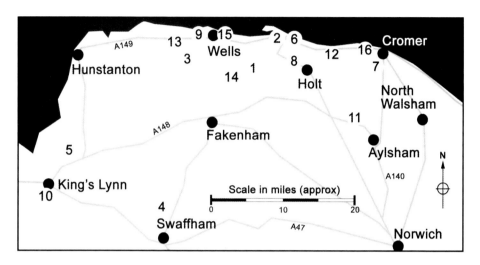

Public Transport

Anglia Railways run trains from Norwich to Cromer, West Runton and Sheringham (The Bittern Line) from where you could connect to Felbrigg (Walk 7), Sheringham Park (Walk 12) and The Roman Camp at West Runton (Walk 16). It is not a frequent service – phone 0845 748 4950 for details.

Trains to King's Lynn are operated by WAGN and run regularly from King's Cross via Cambridge. Castle Rising (Walk 5) would be fairly accessible from King's Lynn, as of course would Walk 10. Phone WAGN on 0845 748 4950.

The North Norfolk Railway runs steam and diesel trains along the 'Poppy Line' from Sheringham to Weybourne and Holt. Phone 01263 822045 for details. The Wells and Walsingham Light Railway is a narrow-gauge steam railway operating during the summer months. Phone their talking timetable on 01328 710631. Both of these railways are essentially tourist services and priced accordingly.

The Coastliner bus service runs along the A149 coast road, connecting with local bus and train services at Hunstanton, Wells, Sheringham and Cromer. There is a limited service to other villages but rural North Norfolk is not easily visited by public transport. Routes and times change constantly. Call the Norfolk Bus Information Centre on 0845 300 6116, Monday to Saturday, 8.00 a.m. to 5.00 p.m.

Bargain priced 'rover' tickets are available on the Coastliner and Bittern Line services. A Sunday Rover gives a day's unlimited travel on bus and train services in Norfolk.

The Country Code

Guard against all risk of fire.

Leave all gates as you find them.

Keep dogs under proper control.

Keep to paths across farmland.

Avoid damaging fences, hedges and walls.

Leave no litter.

Safeguard water supplies.

Protect wildlife, plants and trees.

Go carefully on country roads.

Respect the life of the countryside.

A popular misconception of Norfolk is that it is flat and featureless but I hope that as you follow the walks and explore the places described within this book you will agree that you are discovering a county of great interest and beauty and extraordinary variety.

This is not the landscape of the fens that you would find further West but a gently rolling countryside, pastoral but never cosy, unfolding views of woods and churches and often a glimpse of the sea. Along the 16 walks described here, you will find meandering river valleys, peaceful water meadows and sandy heath. There are ancient woodlands and great landscaped parks. Above all, in this corner of East Anglia you will sense the presence of the sea: even inland in the sharp edge of the wind or a tang of salt in the air. And when you reach the coast itself you will meet a huge variety of scene and mood, from the wilderness of creek and saltmarsh at Blakeney and Cley, to the traditional seaside resorts of Sheringham and Wells, to the sheer magnificence of Holkham Gap.

Within this book you will also find walks that take you out of the countryside to explore the ancient streets of King's Lynn or the pilgrimage village of Walsingham. There are great castles to discover at Castle Acre and Castle Rising and there is the memorable beauty of Binham Priory.

Given the nature of the East Anglian countryside none of these walks involves any real difficulty. We know from experience that all but the two or three longest are manageable with a five-year-old and a baby in a backpack. But bear in mind that walking on sand or shingle can be surprisingly tiring, especially in a strong wind. You won't encounter mountain weather but you still need to respect the elements, especially along the coast. If you plan a coastal walk check the tides first: tide tables are available at newsagents in seaside villages or ring a Tourist Information Centre. Do not wander on to the marshes and sandflats at places such as Blakeney or Wells – tides and currents are fast and it can be extremely dangerous.

You won't need special equipment to complete these walks. Good walking shoes, wellies or trainers are fine for footwear, and a small rucksack is useful to carry waterproofs and food supplies. Lots of small snacks can be helpful, especially towards the end of a walk when children might need extra encouragement and incentives. In summer weather take hats and sun cream, especially on coastal walks where there is little shade. Winter winds can be icy so warm clothes and headgear are essential in the colder months, while the British climate means waterproofs are advisable at any time.

Although we have tried to make the maps as accurate as possible, you would be well advised to take an Ordnance Survey map too on any woodland walks. It is often difficult to determine the route of a path in a wood – and even more difficult to describe it. Foxes and badgers can also create tracks and these change over time, making it hard to map a reliable route. A compass would be extremely useful on any of the walks as directions are often given as compass points.

Refreshments are available at a pub or a café on almost all of the walks and, where possible, this is roughly halfway along the route.

Summary

This is a fairly high and exposed spot on the chalk downs and the delightful views of gently rolling farmland belie the notion that Norfolk is entirely flat. It is easy walking, mainly on track or very quiet lanes, but this is a route probably best avoided after heavy rain as the River Stiffkey can flood, making it impossible to cross the small footbridge near Fiddler's Hill. The focus of the walk is undoubtedly Binham Priory church and its surrounding ruins: not only should you enter and explore this remarkable building but as you skirt around the valley in which it lies you will enjoy an ever-changing perspective of its place in the landscape.

Attractions

The parish church of Binham – the Priory Church of St Mary and the Holy Cross, to give it its full name – was once the nave of a much larger church that formed part of a Benedictine priory founded in 1091. Even as a mere fifth of the original building it is still an impressive monument. The superb west front which greets your approach is a fine example of the Early English style, unusual in East Anglia where many churches were rebuilt after the 14th century with the profits of the wool trade. Guidebooks are available inside the church for those who wish to take a look at the architectural detail. Others will be happy to stand and enjoy the Priory's combination of grace and power and absorb its spirit of enduring calm in this isolated and windy landscape.

Children may have fun looking for the 'poppyheads' on the pew ends: the term derives from the French *poupée* or doll, and the carved figures include a vicar in his pulpit, a baby in swaddling clothes, a monkey, an eagle, a deer and a squirrel.

Fiddler's Hill is the site of a round barrow – an Early Bronze Age burial mound dating from 2000–1400 BC. The site has never been fully excavated although roadworks at the nearby crossroads in 1933 unearthed three skeletons including those of a girl and a dog – probably buried centuries later at what would have become a holy place. Local legend provides an alternative history of the spot in the tale of an underground tunnel running from Binham Priory to Blakeney Guildhall. The story goes that on its discovery only a fiddler and his dog were brave enough to investigate while the Mayor and Corporation of Blakeney followed his progress above ground, guided only by the distant sound of the violin. At the point where the music stopped it was assumed that the fiddler and his dog had been taken by the devil and the spot was named 'Fiddler's Hill'.

Refreshments

There is one pub – The Chequers – and a general store in Binham. If you wished to break the walk in half, you could start and finish at Fiddler's Hill (where there is a small car park and picnic site), stopping for refreshments and a look at the Priory in Binham.

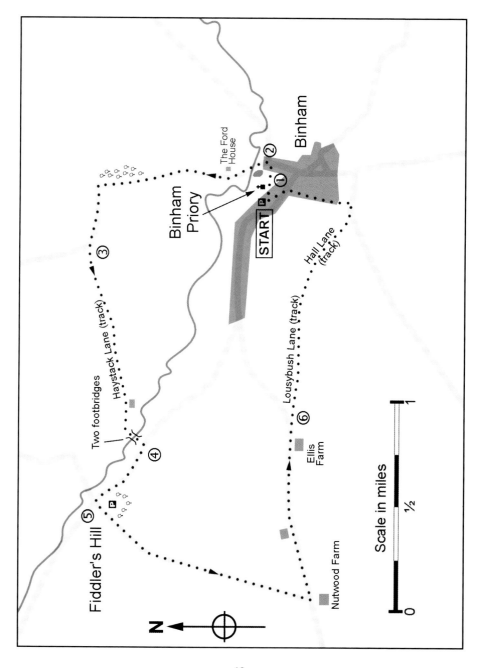

Binham

The Ford House

② Binham

Binham Priory

①

START

Hall Lane (track)

③

Haystack Lane (track)

Two footbridges

④

⑤ Fiddler's Hill

Lousybush Lane (track)

⑥

Ellis Farm

Nutwood Farm

N

Scale in miles

0   ½   1

Start

There is a small car park at the Priory which is in the village of Binham 3 miles north-east of Walsingham. Alternatively you could start at Fiddler's Hill car park and picnic site if you wanted to make Binham your halfway point. O.S. TF 981 399 (Explorer Map 251).

Route

1. Go through the kissing gate at the right-hand corner of the car park as you are facing the Priory Church, then through a second kissing gate into the ruins. Explore the ruins and you will find a third kissing gate to the far right of the open-air altar. Pass through it and then straight across the field to a stile on the right of a pond.
2. Cross the stile and turn left along the lane towards Stiffkey. As you cross Carroll's Bridge over the river, look to your right for a sight of some rather unusual animals! Pass The Ford House and continue for $\frac{1}{2}$ mile to the top of the hill where the lane takes a sharp left-hand turn. Follow the lane around this corner and for a further $\frac{1}{4}$ mile.
3. At a sharp right-hand bend leave the road and follow the Public Footpath sign straight on down a track. Continue along Haystack Lane for $\frac{1}{2}$ mile until you reach a solitary house on your left. Cross the stile and go straight on over the field with the river to your left. Turn left over two footbridges and straight on to another stile. These meadows flood after prolonged or heavy rain – be warned!
4. Cross the stile on to the road, turn right and continue about $\frac{1}{4}$ mile to the crossroads where a left turn will take you to the ancient burial mound of Fiddler's Hill. There is a small car park and picnic site here.
5. From Fiddler's Hill continue southwards along a straight road for about a mile until you come to the T- junction at Nutwood Farm. Turn left here and continue for another $\frac{3}{4}$ mile past two more farms.
6. Shortly after passing Ellis Farm on your right follow the footpath sign into the field in front of you where the road bends away to the left. Bear left along the fence and then follow the direction of the white arrow at the corner to cut across the field. Aim towards a whitish post to meet a grassy track known as Lousybush Lane. Follow this path straight on, crossing the stream (where it becomes Hall Lane) and after $\frac{3}{4}$ mile you will reach the road. Turn left and then left again just past the village sign for Binham to follow a footpath which runs parallel to the main village street and emerges opposite the Priory. Cross the road, pass through the metal gate immediately opposite; the stile taking you back into the car park is across the field to your left.

Summary

The walk begins and ends along the sea wall overlooking Morston saltmarshes while footpaths inland provide fine views to Blakeney Point. Good birdwatching opportunities combine with the chance to explore the village of Blakeney.

Attractions

Blakeney is arguably the most delightful village in Norfolk, with its lanes of flint cottages running down to a picturesque quay and its views out across the saltmarshes to the extraordinary natural feature of Blakeney Point. This 3½-mile-long sand and shingle spit is one of Britain's most important bird sanctuaries and the first nature reserve in Norfolk, noted for its colonies of terns and winter and summer migrants, including oystercatchers and redshanks. It is reached by ferry from Morston or Blakeney from where boat trips can also be taken to see the colonies of grey and common seals around the Point. (Trips run all year, weather permitting. Bean's Boat Trips: 01263 740038 or 740505; Temple Ferry Service: 01263 740791; Bishop's Boats: 01263 740753.) It is highly dangerous to attempt to walk out to the Point from Blakeney but it is possible to walk along the spit from Cley beach to the east. It is an arduous seven miles for the return journey and not recommended for little legs! There is a National Trust information centre at Morston Quay which provides more detail on the area's natural history. A short detour along the route will take in the Church of St Nicholas in Blakeney, supposedly unique in having two towers. The smaller, east tower is believed to have served as a lighthouse guiding ships into the harbour: Blakeney was a flourishing port until the 1900s as witnessed by the 15th century guildhall near the quay of which only the undercroft, with its 13th century vaulting, now remains.

Look out for the plaque on the wall by the quay just before you pass the Blakeney Hotel, which marks the rather alarming height of the 1953 and 1978 floods.

If it is summer and high tide equip yourself with string, a bucket and butcher's scraps and join the children 'crabbing' alongside the creek.

Refreshments

Good selection of pubs, hotels and teashops in Blakeney. The Anchor Public House in Morston also sells tickets for boat trips.

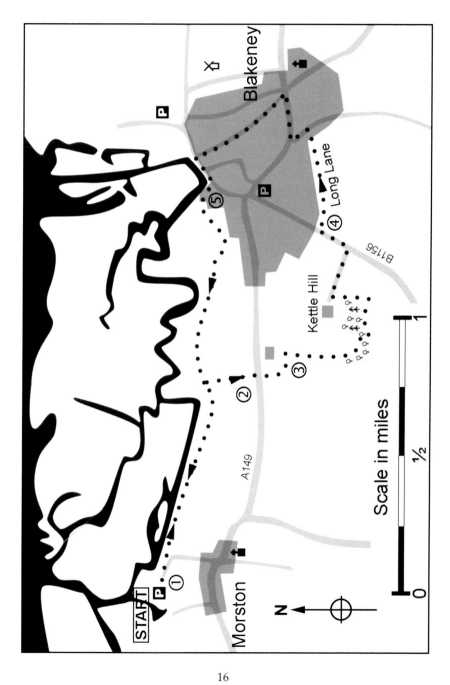

Blakeney

Long Lane

B1156

Kettle Hill

Morston

A149

START

Scale in miles

0   ½   1

N

Start

At Morston, 6 miles east of Wells-next-the-Sea on the A149 coast road. Follow signs for the Quay from the centre of the village and park in car park by visitor centre. (National Trust members free – display membership card on windscreen; Pay and Display machine at Observation Gallery.) O.S. TG 006 442 (Explorer Map 251).

Route

1. Follow footpath sign to the right of the Public Observation Gallery eastwards along the sea wall, towards the tower of Blakeney church in the distance. After ⅓ mile descend a flight of wooden steps and after another 30 yards take a path to the right heading inland between a hedge on your left and a few houses on your right.
2. When you reach the main road turn right and walk with care for 50 yards (the traffic here is fast). Then cross the main road by the entrance to 'Northdown' and take the public footpath through the five-bar gate.
3. Follow the path round the base of the hill on which stands a large thatched house and then turn right and follow the path southwards towards a small wood, keeping a hedge on your right. When you reach the wood bear left along the path which skirts its north side, keeping the trees on your right. After 50 yards turn right through a small gap in the wood and then almost immediately left. Follow the wooden fence which bounds the large private garden of Kettle Hill, taking a left turn at the corner, until you reach the main entrance drive. Follow the footpath as it turns right down this tarmac drive away from the house.
4. When you reach the road turn left towards Blakeney. After 100 yards and immediately before the first houses on the outskirts of the village, take a footpath to your right marked 'Long Lane'. Follow the path round to the left through a thicket until it emerges on to a track. Continue straight on between a few houses on to a lane, turn left and after 50 yards you will reach the main road. Turn right and walk for 100 yards along this road (there is a pavement). The first turn on your left will take you down the high street to Blakeney village and quay. If you wish to visit the church, turn right at this junction.
5. When you are ready to complete the walk, find the footpath sign at the west end of Blakeney quay at the bend of the creek. It is by the seaward corner of an impressive red-brick house. Here you will emerge again on to the saltmarshes and will be able to see the Public Observation Gallery at Morston in the distance. Follow the sea wall back to Morston quay.

Summary

Burnham Thorpe is chiefly remarkable for being the birthplace of Admiral Lord Nelson and this walk takes in the site of his birth, the parish church where his father was rector and the pub in which he drank. The walk begins and ends on village lanes while the middle mile or two is on good level track across rolling farmland with lovely views north towards the sea. A short detour towards the end of the walk takes you over and along the River Burn to reach the site of Nelson's birthplace. There is a good playground on the village green which should revive the tiredest five-year-old.

Attractions

Burnham Thorpe is the easternmost of what were originally the seven 'Burnhams' – prosperous villages less than a mile apart, each with a fine medieval church. Today Burnham Market is a delightful large village while Burnham Overy has its Staithe or harbour, but of the Burnhams Deepdale, Norton, Westgate and Sutton, maybe a church is all that remains. The villages are worth exploring, none the less, and by combining this walk with Walk 13, you could include all seven.

> *'Probably I shall never see dear dear Burnham again but I have a satisfaction in thinking that my bones will probably be laid with my father's in the village that gave me birth.'*

So wrote Admiral Nelson in 1804 from HMS *Victory*. Sadly, he was in fact buried in St Paul's Cathedral but the bones of his brother and sister, as well as those of his father, lie at All Saints Church in Burnham Thorpe. His father was rector of All Saints – or 'Nelson's Church' – and Horatio was born in the old Rectory (since demolished and replaced) though local legend has it that his mother in fact gave birth in the huge flint barn beside the inn, having gone into labour while out on a drive in a pony cart.

Before you enter the church, look to see if the White Ensign is flying from the tower; if not, you should find it inside. The flag has no St Patrick's cross because it predates the Union of England and Ireland in 1801 and is a replica of one flown at the Battle of the Nile. All Saints Church is almost unique in being granted the right by the British Admiralty to fly it. You will find other Nelson memorabilia in the church, including flags from HMS *Indomitable* flown at the Battle of Jutland. The cross above the rood beam over the chancel arch and the lectern were both made from timbers from HMS *Victory*, certified as such by the Admiralty who donated them.

Despite having such a famous son, Burnham Thorpe is remarkably untouched by the tourist industry: the site of his birthplace is marked only by a small plaque. The original Rectory has been demolished and it is not possible to visit the grounds or see the pond that Nelson himself is supposed to have dug while staying in Burnham Thorpe; he spent a five-year period, with no ship to command and on half-pay, living with his father at the Rectory.

Before taking command of his new ship – the *Agamemnon* – in 1793, Nelson is said

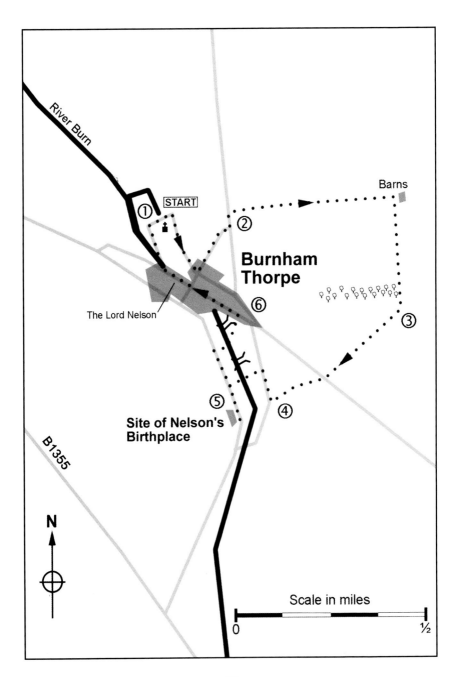

START

Barns

River Burn

① ②

Burnham
Thorpe

The Lord Nelson

⑥

③

⑤

④

Site of Nelson's
Birthplace

B1355

N

Scale in miles

0   ½

to have held a farewell party for the villagers in the Lord Nelson Inn, then known as The Plough and renamed in 1807, two years after his death. The pub, which dates back to the 1650s, must be little changed since Nelson drank there and is worth a visit for more Nelson paintings and memorabilia (some for sale) and for the world-famous secret recipe of Nelson's Blood!

Refreshments

A visit to the Lord Nelson Inn is almost an essential part of this walk. Known as 'The pub with no bar' (it really hasn't), it is an historic inn with stone-flagged floors and original wooden settles. Families are welcome and there is a large garden and children's play area. There is a wide choice of snacks or larger meals.

Start

In the village of Burnham Thorpe, 2 miles south of the A149 coast road between Wells-next-the-Sea and Brancaster. Park by the church which is off a lane at the north-east corner of the village. O.S. TF 851 418 (Explorer Map 251).

Route

1. With your back to the church bear right along the lane and continue round the bend to your right and down the lane until you reach a crossroads. Turn left here by the village hall and head out of the village, bearing right at the bend.
2. At the T-junction turn left and after 100 yards take the track to your right to head across the field towards a group of old barns. When you reach the barns turn right again and follow the track up towards the wood. (As you pass the end of the wood it is worth pausing to look behind you and admire the view.)
3. At the next T-junction of the paths bear right and follow the track down the hill until you reach the road, which you should cross to continue on the track immediately opposite.
4. When you reach the next road turn right along it towards the village but after 100 yards cross over a stile on your left and take the path across the field towards the footbridge. Cross over the stream and turn left to walk along its bank towards another stile. Climb this and turn left and then you will find the site of Nelson's birthplace about 20 yards along the lane.
5. Retrace your steps to head back up the lane towards the village, this time taking the third footpath sign to your right (about $\frac{1}{4}$ mile), just beyond the house called The Shooting Box. Follow the hedge to cross a stile and then take another footbridge back over the river. Head across the field towards some cottages and a large sycamore.
6. When you reach the lane turn left and head into the village. After you have passed the Lord Nelson pub on your left, follow the stream and bear right up the lane towards the church.

Summary

Castle Acre is one of the most historic spots in Norfolk so this is quite a short walk allowing plenty of time to explore the Priory and Castle. The going is easy along footpaths and very quiet lanes but it is a delightful walk through peaceful woodland and along the pretty river valley of the Nar. There are some good views across this open part of Norfolk, particularly from the Castle mound, and of the Priory ruins from the lanes returning you to the village.

Attractions

Castle Acre has been described as the 'greatest place in East Anglia for ruin lovers' but is also a delightful village in its own right with its pretty green and the ancient cottages of Bailey Street running down to the river from an imposing 11th century gateway. The history of Castle Acre may well date back to the Iron Age. By Roman times it was standing at the junction of two important routes, one of which – the Peddar's Way – is now a long-distance footpath running north/south across Norfolk. This walk follows the Peddar's Way for a short distance and also the east/west route known as the Nar Valley Way.

It was as a Norman settlement that Castle Acre really came to prominence and it is still possible to explore some of the most impressive earthworks in the country and the ruins of a great double-moated keep. The village itself would have formed the outer bailey with its Bailey Gate: many of the houses of the village contain flints from the original castle walls.

At the other end of the village lies Britain's best-preserved Cluniac Priory. The Cluniac monasteries of England were established by William de Warenne – a son-in-law of William the Conqueror – and derive from the great abbey at Cluny in Burgundy. Castle Acre was founded as a daughter priory of the first English Cluniac house, at Lewes, and survived a stormy history of conflict between the head of the order in France and the English monarchy, until its dissolution by Henry VIII in 1537.

The abbey church was built in the 11th and 12th centuries and modelled on a church at Cluny; its superb west front still rises to its original height. The fine Tudor house that served as the Prior's lodgings is still intact and contains a private chapel, while it is easy to trace the remains of the cloisters, refectory, dormitory and even the latrines (or *necessarium* as it was euphemistically known).

East of Castle Acre, in the villages of Newton, Great Dunham and the Lexhams, lie four Anglo-Saxon churches, whose escape from Norman rebuilding has never been fully explained. A Saxon burial ground was also discovered in the area in Victorian times: more than 100 urns were unearthed and two great stone coffins found in the River Nar, possibly containing the remains of William de Warenne and his wife Gundreda. The coffins were dragged from the river to the church, on the orders of the rector, but the workmen who carried out this task, disgruntled with what they regarded as inadequate 'beer money', threw the coffins back into the river, where they are assumed to remain today.

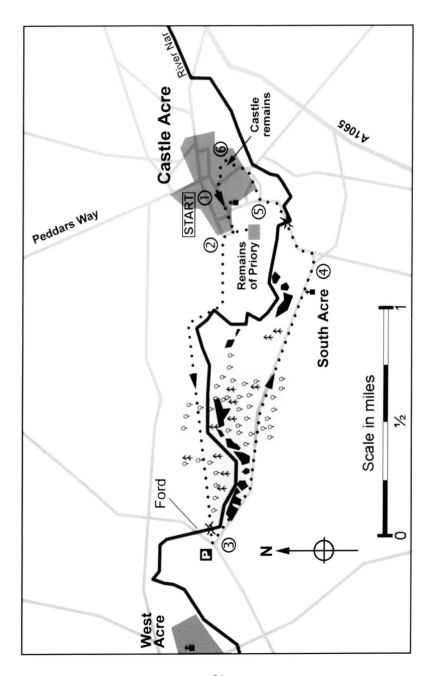

Castle Acre

River Nar

Peddars Way

Castle remains

⑥

START ①

② ⑤

Remains of Priory

A1065

④ South Acre

Ford

P ③

West Acre

N

Scale in miles

0   ½   1

Refreshments

The Albert Victor and The Ostrich are good family pubs with gardens. You will also find a restaurant, a tea room and a village stores on the green. The ford by Mill House would be a perfect spot for a picnic and is about halfway along the route.

Start

In the centre of Castle Acre village which is a mile west of the A1065 and 4 miles north of Swaffham. Park by the village green, near the Post Office. O.S. TF 816 151 (Explorer Map 236).

Route

1. With the Post Office on your left, leave the village green and go straight on down Priory Road, passing the church on your left. Continue straight to the end of the lane and turn left to visit the Priory ruins. Retrace your steps to the corner and now go straight on, heading north.

2. At the next corner take the footpath to your left, following the sign to the Nar Valley Way. Follow the track as it curves to the right and then the left, and where it bends again to the right take the footpath through the kissing gate on your left to follow the river along the Nar Valley Way. After $\frac{1}{2}$ mile pass through another kissing gate into a narrow wood. Continue straight on, crossing a stile by a five-bar gate, to reach two footbridges over the river. Cross the bridges and follow the path straight on up to the road.

3. Turn right if you wish to visit the ford, which would be an enchanting picnic spot. Otherwise, turn left along the lane to reach the corner and then left again along the road to return to Castle Acre on the other side of the river.

4. After $1\frac{1}{2}$ miles the road forks. Take the left-hand fork and follow the lane round to the left past a three-storey flint house (Church Farm). Then curve round to the right and down the hill to cross the footbridge over the stream. Carry straight on up the lane towards the village.

5. After 100 yards turn right and keep right at the bend. When you reach the main road turn left and after 50 yards turn right down Cuckstool Lane. After another 50 yards turn left into the castle earthworks.

6. To return to the starting point of the walk, leave the castle at the north-west corner and turn right up the hill along Bailey Street. Pass under the Bailey Gate arch and then turn left towards the village green.

Summary

This is a short and gentle walk on level path and track. There is no road walking but you do have to cross the A149 – twice, unfortunately – which can be difficult at very busy times: perhaps this walk is best avoided at peak holiday periods. Away from the main road, however, this is attractive and peaceful farmland and there are splendid views from the castle mound. The keep is one of the largest in the country and worth exploring, as is the pretty village. The walk takes in a small corner of a much larger wood and for half a mile or so runs along the banks of the Babingley River.

Attractions

Rising was a sea-port when Lynn was but a marsh
Now Lynn is the sea-port and Rising fares the worse.

The earthworks of Castle Rising testify to its importance in Roman and Norman times – and maybe even earlier – when it stood very close to the sea on the Babingley estuary and could have become as great a port as King's Lynn had the waters of the Wash not receded some four or five miles.

There is still much to see of the great Norman castle. The hall keep (as opposed to a tower keep, because it is wider than it is high) has been well preserved, retaining two storeys of intact rooms and some fine decoration. Amongst the earthworks to the north archaeologists discovered the foundations of a chapel, now known to be of Saxon origin. The keep is second in importance only to Norwich Castle and its history is, inevitably, a chequered one. It was built in about 1150 by William D'Albini, son of another William who was butler to William the Conqueror from whom he had received the site as a gift. It later passed through the ownership of the Crown before returning in the 16th century to Thomas Howard, Duke of Norfolk, who could trace his ancestry to this same butler. Between 1331 and 1356 it served as a kind of open prison for Queen Isabella who was banished there by her son Edward III for suspected complicity in the murder of his father.

Just off the route of this walk, across the road from the church, is the Hospital of the Holy and Undivided Trinity founded in 1614 by Henry Howard, the Earl of Northampton, to provide homes for 'twelve poor women'. These almshouses still function today and the present inhabitants process to church wearing their tradi-tional red cloaks with the Howard badge and their steeple hats. Whether they all comply with the strict qualifications laid down by the founder is anyone's guess!

'... of honest life and conversation, religious, grave and discreet, able to read if such a one may be had, single, 56 at least, no common beggar, harlot, scold, drunkard, haunter of taverns, inns or alehouses.'

If you visit the 12th century church , much restored by the Victorians, take a look at the evil, leering faces on the west side of the font.

As you pass along the edge of Castle Rising wood you may detect the smell of wild garlic – abundant here apparently and giving rise to the name of Onion Corner.

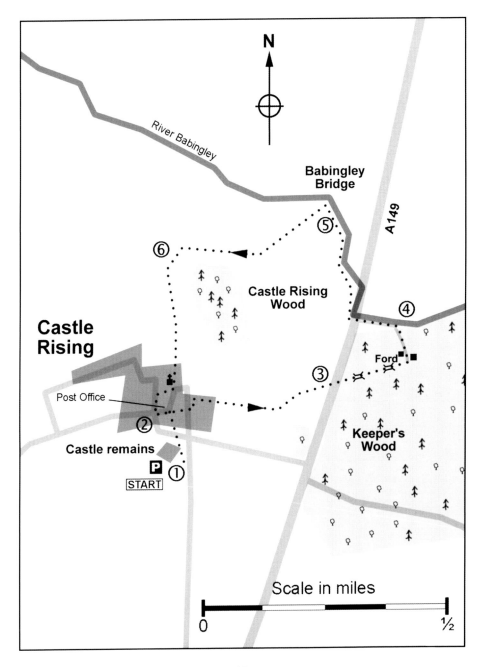

N

River Babingley

Babingley
Bridge

A149

⑤

⑥

Castle Rising
Wood

Castle
Rising

④

⑶

Ford

Post Office

②

Keeper's
Wood

Castle remains

P
START ①

Scale in miles

0 ½

Refreshments

The post office stores in the village serves teas. Next door is the Black Horse Inn.

Start

Castle Rising is situated 1 mile north of the roundabout linking the A148 and the A149 at the north-west corner of King's Lynn. Although only a small village, Castle Rising has its own one-way system. Follow the signs from the A149 to park in the castle car park. The ruins are owned by English Heritage and there is a fee to visit the castle, but parking is free and it is not necessary to enter the castle in order to complete the walk. O.S. TF 667 245 (Explorer Map 250).

Route

1. Walk from the car park towards the kiosk and shop where you can buy tickets to visit the castle if you wish. Take the footpath that runs past the castle entrance towards the village. Cross the road to reach the pavement and then turn left and walk to the crossroads where you will see the Post Office, shop and tea room.
2. Turn right and then take the footpath on the corner by the large lamp-post, opposite the Black Horse Inn. Cross the next road and turn left and then right after 20 yards to take a footpath (signed on other side of road), passing allotments on your left and a large oak tree on your right. Continue straight on up the next field, keeping the hedge on your left, and then bear slightly to your left, again keeping the hedge on your left, to cross the next field and reach the road.
3. Cross the A149 with great care and take the signed footpath into the woods a few yards to your left. Follow the path, crossing a little bridge over the stream and bear left and then straight on through the woods, fording another stream, to reach some houses. At the signpost at the corner of the *Leylandii* hedge turn left and then left again along the metalled drive. When you reach the corner take the signed footpath immediately opposite you across the field to reach the Babingley River.
4. Turn left and walk along the bank of the stream, passing beneath a large beech and crossing a stile to reach the main road again. Cross the road and continue to follow the stream until you reach a track at Babingley Bridge.
5. Turn left and follow the metalled track to the far corner of Castle Rising Wood. Here the track bends to the left around the wood. Take the signed footpath to continue straight on down a slight hill and then 200 yards along the field edge to reach another track.
6. Turn left down the track and, after passing two houses, follow it round to the right and then take a left turn to bring you back to the village via the church and post office.

The homeward stretch: Hurdle Lane near Cley next the Sea

Summary

This is a walk of much variety. It starts and ends in the village of Cley but in between includes marsh and beach, heath and farmland. Most of the walk is on footpaths, initially along the sea wall. You could opt to walk along the shingle beach for half a mile instead of taking the path, which is a few yards inland. There is a little road walking but it is mostly on very quiet lanes with the exception of a 50-yard stretch along the A149 Coast Road which requires care.

Attractions

Cley Marshes are famed internationally as one of the finest bird habitats in Britain and much of this walk is on land owned by three conservation bodies: The Norfolk Naturalists Trust, the National Trust and the Norfolk Ornithologists Association. Whatever the season, whatever the weather, ornithologists and amateur birdwatchers can be found enjoying this landscape and its wildlife. The huge skies, the shifting light on the water, the wind in the reeds and the plaintive cries of the seabirds: the very essence of the North Norfolk coast is here at Cley. In spring the easiest birds to spot are probably the avocets with their striking black and white plumage and graceful up-curving beaks. In summer redshanks are recognisable by their distinctive red legs, and as autumn progresses ducks and Brent geese return to their Winter feeding grounds. The prize sighting, however, has to be that of the elusive bittern, of which only a handful of pairs are breeding in East Anglian reserves. You may hear its distinctive booming call on summer evenings, but we were rewarded with a close-up view when rehearsing this walk. For access to the marshes themselves and the hides you will need a permit, obtainable for a small fee from the Visitor Centre, where you can also hire binoculars. Tel. 01263 740008.

The village of Cley has some handsome houses, many showing a Dutch influence, and picturesque lanes – or lokes – of flint and brick, colourful with hollyhocks in summer. The 18th century Custom House and St Margaret's church –– its interior one great impression of space and light – are evidence that, like many Norfolk villages, Cley was once a thriving port, its fortune derived from the export of Norfolk wool to Europe in the 14th century. The advent of the Black Death and changes in the wool trade marked the start of its decline and the intended great west tower of the church was never built. The silting-up of the Glaven estuary eventually made the harbour redundant and brought to an end Cley's Golden Age.

Cley mudflats are a good source of samphire or poor man's asparagus (also known as glasswort, saltwort, pickle plant or crab-grass). It is a fleshy plant with wiry stems and has been compared to a forest of miniature trees sprouting from the mud. From June to September you can buy it from roadside stalls or local fishmongers along this stretch of coast or pick it yourself at low tide. Look for good bushy plants, cut with a sharp knife just above the base and wash very well in cold water. Steam or boil the plants for five minutes and serve like asparagus with melted butter, drawing the stems between your teeth to remove the succulent tips.

Refreshments

There is a choice of pubs and tea shops in Cley, or stock up in the village shop and picnic on Salthouse Heath looking down to the sea. In high season teas and coffees are available at the car park by Cley beach and at the Cley Marshes Visitor Centre.

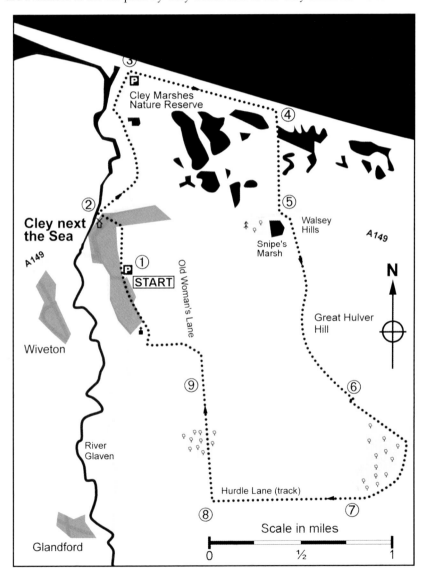

Cley next the Sea 6 *miles*

Cley next the Sea - Cley Marshes
- Salthouse Heath - Cley next the Sea

6

Start

In the village of Cley next the Sea. Park in the car park beside the village hall which is signposted from the Holt Road. O.S. TG 047 437 (Explorer Map 251).

Route

1. Turn right out of the car park and take the lane past two entrances to Cley Hall. Go down the track, passing the old school building on your left and turn left in front of The Old Manor House. Turn right down the alley marked to Cley Mill and High Street. Cross the road and take the track immediately opposite you towards the windmill. Enter a small courtyard with the windmill on your left and you will find the footpath in the right-hand corner of the courtyard. Climb the steps over the wall and turn right along the edge of the reed bed to reach the sea wall.
2. Ascend to the top of the sea wall and then head along it towards the sea.
3. When you reach the sea walk eastwards, either along the beach itself or along the path that runs just inland behind the shingle bank.
4. After ¾ mile, turn right and walk along the bank away from the sea.
5. When you reach the road, turn left and walk along the grass verge for 50 yards (take care). Cross the road to the lay-by just beyond the pond known as Snipe's Marsh and take the footpath marked to Salthouse and Salthouse Heath. Ignore the steps to your left and go straight on along the path. At the next junction go straight on again, following signs to Salthouse Heath and not left to Salthouse. Continue up the hill, passing Great Hulver Hill on your left.
6. You will emerge on the road at a Y-shaped junction. Turn neither immediately right nor left but cross the first road and the grass and take the next left-hand fork, signed to Bodham and Gresham. Walk alongside the wood for ¼ mile to the crossroads and then turn right towards Holt and Norwich. Continue skirting the wood until you come to a T-junction.
7. Cross the road and take a wide track marked as a public footpath (Hurdle Lane).
8. After half a mile you will emerge on to the road at a sharp bend. Turn right down the footpath that runs along the edge of the field. Pass through a 'doorway' in the hedge and then go down and up the next field and straight on through the wood. Emerge from the wood on to heathland and follow the path down the hill and into a field. Continue following the path along the hedge down to the road.
9. Cross the road and take the track immediately opposite into the field, through the copse and down to the next road. Turn left and follow the road past Old Woman's Lane on your right and back towards the village. Just before you reach the Green, turn right up Church Lane to return to the car park.

Summary

This walk is contained entirely within the Felbrigg Estate, now owned by the National Trust. The woodland, lakeside walk and parkland are open every day of the year except Christmas day from dawn till dusk, free of charge. The walk is entirely on footpaths apart from a small section at the end along the main driveway of The Hall where traffic is not heavy, except perhaps on bank holiday afternoons. It begins and ends in ancient woodland, taking in parkland, lakeside and the parish church along the way. The walk could easily be combined with a visit to Felbrigg Hall – one of the finest 17th century houses in East Anglia – and its walled garden. For opening times and prices contact the National Trust (tel. 01263 837444). The walk is essentially a figure-of-eight and is easily divided into two separate shorter walks.

Attractions

Felbrigg Hall, an important 17th century house with later additions, lies at the centre of 1700 acres of woods and parkland on the Cromer Ridge. The glacial origins of this undulating terrain, sculpted 12,000 years ago by ice sheets and melt water, are clearly visible in the steep-sided Foxburrow Valley through which your path will cross. But manmade influences on this landscape are perhaps more readily apparent. The Great Wood, for example, was at least in part the creation of William Windham I, who inherited Felbrigg in 1665, although the existence of certain lichens on the barks of the ancient trees testifies to the primeval origins of the woodland. Windham was one of the first Englishmen to create plantations. A typical entry in his ledger from 1676 records:

> *'I paled the Nurserye, (which I hope will be carefully preserved so long as it please God to continue it in the ffamily), & did then sow there 6 comb of Acorns: 1 Comb of Ashe Keys: 1 Comb of Haws: 2 bushells of Holly Berryes: 1500 Chestnuts: 1 bushell of Maple & Sycamore Keys & a very few Beech Mast. I did then plant 4000 Oaks; 800 Ashes: 600 Birches: 70 Beeches: & 50 Crabs which were all small.'*

Many fine specimens of ancient sweet chestnut and beech remain, the latter supposedly at the limit of its native range, but there is also a large variety of conifers including specimens of the world's two tallest life forms – the redwood and the Douglas fir. Many of the conifers were planted this century by Felbrigg's last private owner, the distinguished historian R. W. Kremer, who left the Hall and estate to the National Trust in 1969. His most distinctive contribution was probably the Victory Wood planted at the end of the Second World War around a pair of rides that meet to form a V for Victory. On a clear day it should be possible to see the spire of Norwich cathedral, some 20 miles distant, from the apex of the V.

The landscaped park was largely a late 18th century creation, typical of its time and the naturalistic fashion associated with 'Capability' Brown and Humphrey Repton, with its broad views and informal grouping of trees. Repton, who designed the nearby Sheringham Park (see Walk 12) and who is buried in Aylsham church-yard, lived for a time at nearby Sustead. No one seems sure whether he was

35

involved in the design of Felbrigg park or was himself influenced by it.

At the time of the creation of the park, a series of old fishponds, once stocked with tench and carp, was damned to form a more impressive lake. Along with its reedbeds this is now an important wetland habitat, home to 50 different plant species – though no rarities. Look out for common spotted orchids and marsh marigolds. In early summer you should hear – and spot if you are lucky – sedge warblers and willow tits. You will have no trouble sighting the flock of Canada geese that roosts here in winter.

Refreshments

The Park Restaurant and Turret Tea-Room open the same days and times as The Hall. Check first if refreshments are vital (01263 838237).

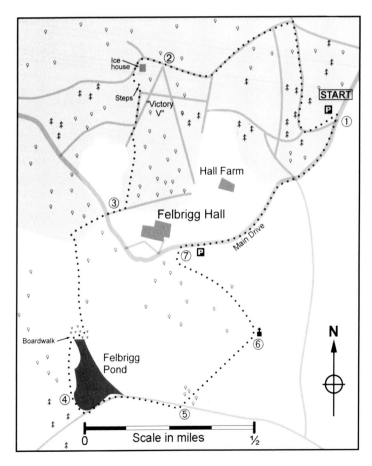

Start

At the 'Dog-walkers car park' on the edge of Felbrigg Woods. Take the main entrance to Felbrigg Hall off the B1436 1 mile south of the A148 between Sheringham and Cromer and follow the first car park sign $\frac{1}{3}$ mile along the entrance drive to your right. O.S. TG 202 401 (Explorer Map 252).

Route

1. From the car park follow the path into the woods, taking a right-hand turn after 50 yards. At the crossroads turn left and continue straight or rightish, ignoring any turns to your left, until you reach the Victory V viewpoint – the apex of two long avenues cut through the trees and forming a V-shape, with a bench at the point where the two arms meet.

2. From the Victory V take the path leading straight up from the point of the V (behind you as you sit on the bench) and then turn left at the marker post by another bench. Immediately after you have passed the ice house, the path forks. Keep to the left and then turn left again 25 yards from the fork to enter the woods. Go down and then up the steps and turn right at the top to meet the westward arm of the Victory V. Cross over the avenue to the left-hand five-bar gate and go through it into the wooded part of the deer park. Follow the path along the side of the fence until you reach a track, then turn right and through the five-bar gate to bring you on to the main drive. If you wish to break up the walk at this point, you can turn left to bring you to Felbrigg Hall and Garden. Refreshments are available at the tea room and restaurant. Alternatively you could turn right along the drive to reach the picnic area (about 100 yards).

3. Cross the drive and take the path following signs marked 'Weavers' Way'. Keep the fence on your left and at the corner bear left to follow the track between two wire fences, turn right at the corner and then go down the hill and over the boardwalk through reedbeds, remaining between the two fences. Continue to follow markers for the Weavers' Way, following the path straight on and then round to your left at the top of the field. Pass through the gate and over the boardwalk to reach the lake.

4. Follow the path around the southern side of the lake. At its southernmost tip leave the Weavers' Way, which branches off to your right, and continue to follow the path around the lake. At its easternmost point pass through a five-bar gate and take the path up a hill, keeping the fence on your left.

5. At the top of the hill, where there are two pollarded beech trees and some new planting, turn left through a gate by one of the beeches and strike out across the field towards the church.

6. Explore the church if you wish. Then go through a gate at the corner of the church-yard wall and follow the path back in the direction of the Hall.

7. When you reach the main drive, turn right and after $\frac{1}{2}$ mile you will reach on your left the car park where you started your walk.

Summary

This is mainly gentle walking on footpath and track although there is quite a steep climb (by Norfolk standards) at the end to return you to the starting point on Wiveton Down. There is a one-mile stretch of very quiet lane (tractors are the most likely traffic you'll encounter). Glandford Shell Museum and the 'Natural Surroundings' wildlife centre are both well worth a visit.

This walk is included by kind permission of Robin Combe and the Bayfield Estate. Most of the paths are not actually public rights of way and walkers are requested to observe all signs, close gates where necessary and respect the ecologically sensitive areas. The estate owners would be very grateful to hear of any sightings of water voles, Little Owls, otters or, particularly, mink (01263 712219).

Attractions

The starting point of this walk, at Wiveton Downs, offers wonderful views towards the sea and also inland over the peaceful valley of the River Glaven. The walk is almost entirely on land belonging to the Bayfield Estate whose present owners welcome careful walkers although Bayfield Hall (of Elizabethan origins) is not open to the public. The estate (Bayfelda in the Domesday book) was sold to the Jodrell family in 1776 with whom it remained until 1929 when it passed to the Coke family of Holkham fame. The village of Glandford is largely the work of Sir Alfred Jodrell who commissioned the Flemish-style estate cottages and the church at the turn of the century. The church, built in memory of Sir Alfred's mother, has some notable features, including its carved pew ends: look for the dog grieving over its master's coffin, derived from the painting by Landseer entitled *The Shepherd's Chief Mourner*. Sir Alfred also created the Glandford Shell Museum to house his collection of shells and artefacts from all over the world. It makes a curious and fascinating diversion if you are here between Easter and October when it is open Tuesday to Saturday and Bank Holidays. Phone 01263 740081 for details.

The Jodrell family were also responsible for landscaping Bayfield lake although it had been created from the River Glaven at an earlier date. The ancient woods and parkland contain a number of venerable trees, including at least one Elizabethan oak in the meadow beside the lake. In May the woods are a mass of bluebells. Today the park provides a valuable habitat for barn owls, badgers and otters: the latter were introduced on to the estate in the 1980s, bred successfully and now flourish though you would be very lucky to see one in daylight. Four varieties of bat have colonized the old tunnel, built to prevent silting of the lake and running parallel to it.

Hidden away in the woods is 'Natural Surroundings', a centre for wildlife gardening and conservation. The meadows and nursery, organic gardens and woodland trail are open every weekend and Bank Holiday, except for Christmas and New Year, and on some weekdays. Special events such as country crafts workshops, nightingale rambles and raft races are also organised throughout the year. Phone 01263 711091 for details.

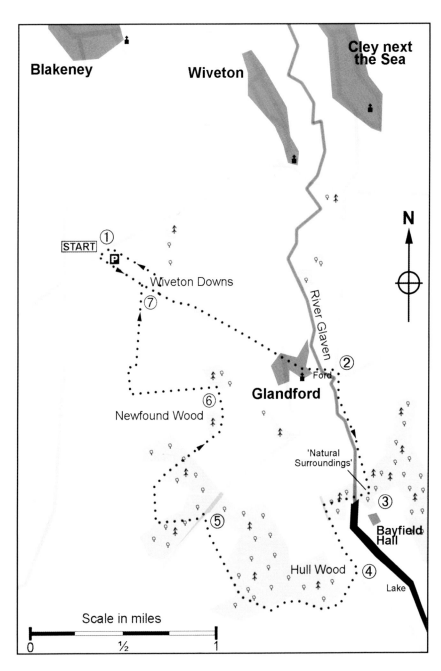

Blakeney

Wiveton

Cley next
the Sea

N

START ①

Wiveton Downs

⑦

River Glaven

② Ford

Glandford

⑥
Newfound Wood

'Natural
Surroundings'

③

Bayfield
Hall

⑤

Hull Wood ④

Lake

Scale in miles

0   ½   1

Refreshments

There is a tea room at Natural Surroundings, open the same times as the wildflower centre. Wiveton Downs has a picnic site near the car park. Holt and Blakeney offer a wide choice of restaurants, pubs and shops.

Start

Park at the car park at Wiveton Downs, one mile south of Blakeney. From the A149 coast road take the Saxlingham Road out of Blakeney. From Holt take the A148 westwards, then the Blakeney Road from Letheringsett and turn left at Glandford for Wiveton Downs. O.S. TG 032 423 (Explorer Map 251).

Route

1. Walk back out of the car park on to the road and turn left. Take the next left turn and continue along this lane for ¾ mile, then cross the road into the village of Glandford. Pass the church on your right and at the ford follow the footpath over the bridge.
2. Where the road forks bear right and at the end of the flint wall go through the gate on your right and take the footpath to follow the course of the river. After ½ mile enter the woods through the five-bar gate and continue straight on to 'Natural Surroundings' countryside centre.
3. Turn right at 'Natural Surroundings' to go straight down the main drive, passing the lake and the weir on your left and crossing the stream. Twenty yards short of the main gates turn left off the drive into the woods, following the footpath sign. Cross the barbed wire fence by means of the metal ladder, turn right and then follow the path along the park wall. Please keep close to the wall so as not to disturb nesting wildfowl. After ¼ mile leave the park through the gate and cross the road with care.
4. Take the track immediately opposite to skirt Hull Wood. Bear right at the first fork and left at the next to continue along the edge of the wood. Then follow the next track up the hill and into the wood, keeping the two silver birches (at time of writing) on your left. (The public footpath continues straight on at this point.) Continue on this path as the woods open out and then carry straight on to the road, keeping the woods on your right.
5. Turn left along the road and then right, after 20 yards, along the track. At the top of the hill turn right along the edge of the field. At the next corner follow the track through the woods and then straight on down the field. Bear left to skirt around Newfound Wood. At the next corner take the path straight on rather than following the track to your right towards Glandford.
6. Turn left along the next track you meet and then right at the next. Continue straight on until you reach the road.
7. Turn right along the road and where it starts to bend follow a path through a small gap in the hedge on your left (200 yards). Climb to the top of the hill and then turn left up the steps to the bench. Follow the path back to the car park.

Summary

While probably the toughest walk in the book, this boasts, to my mind, some of the most glorious landscapes in Norfolk. It is also a walk of contrasts: between the remote wilderness of dune and marsh and the tamed classical beauty of a great landscaped park. The two miles of beach walking are strenuous, particularly in a high wind, but the gentle paths of Holkham Park then come as a relief. The walk is completed – unavoidably – along roads with one short stretch (¾ mile) requiring some care, although traffic is very light except in the height of the summer.

Before starting this walk, it is essential to consider two things – the weather conditions and the tide. In a strong easterly wind, you might do well to keep the wind behind you along the beach by walking the route anticlockwise, although the disadvantage is that you will be confronted with two miles of sand at the end of the walk when you may be tired. Starting from Lady Ann's Drive is another option but there would be nowhere to stop for food or drink until the end of the walk. You should only attempt this walk on an ebb tide, aiming to reach Holkham Gap at low water. Although the route runs consistently above the mean high water mark, tides along this coast are unpredictable and sometimes dangerous.

Attractions

The centrepiece of this walk is the great classical mansion of Holkham Hall – severe and forbidding perhaps, but to its admirers one of the finest examples of the Palladian style. The Hall and its vast landscaped park were the creation of Thomas Coke, the First Earl of Leicester who, like other English aristocrats, found his inspiration in Italy while on a Grand Tour. Coke's main aim in building the Hall was to house the works of art he had accumulated on the Continent. Sadly he died in 1762 after many decades of work but before the building was complete.

The park and gardens were the work of William Kent and 'Capability' Brown. Some of their most distinctive features are the grand avenues and clumps of evergreen or holm oak, whose origins may also lie in The Grand Tour: the antique statues in the sculpture gallery are said to have been packed in the seeds of *Quercus ilex* which may well have been put to good use in the grounds.

The name 'Coke of Norfolk' became famous during the agricultural revolution as applied to the great-nephew of the First Earl. By applying the ideas of 'Turnip' Townshend of nearby Raynham Hall as well as many of his own innovations, rotation farming in particular, he made enormous improvements to the fertility of his land. The barn where he held his annual sheep-shearing is still standing, as is the great memorial column to the north of the house, erected by his neighbours on his death. Domestic animals decorate the plinth and the top is crowned with a wheatsheaf.

Enjoy the coastal section of this walk for its vast and lonely sands and the great East Anglian skyscape. But keep a look-out at your feet too for evidence of Norfolk's

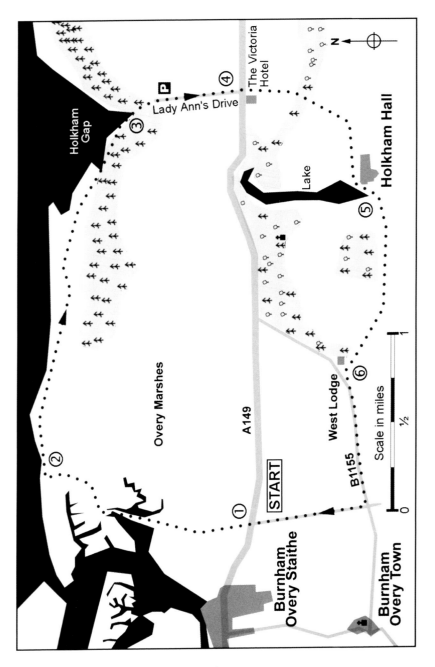

Holkham Gap

The Victoria Hotel

Lady Ann's Drive

④

③

N

Holkham Hall

Lake

⑤

Overy Marshes

A149

West Lodge

⑥

Scale in miles

B1155

②

START ①

Burnham Overy Staithe

Burnham Overy Town

0   ½   1

abundant shellfish. West of Holkham, at Brancaster Staithe, are excellent mussel and oyster beds, and to the east at Stiffkey and Wells are the finest cockles or 'Stewkey Blues' (because of their blue-black shells). Here at Holkham you may find the shells of Norfolk razor-shell clams. These are said to be delicious but collecting them is not easy because of the speed with which they can burrow deep into the sand at the sea's edge. Look out for a pair of small holes and a pattern of splash marks, then dig quickly and carefully with a small trowel.

Refreshments

The Victoria Hotel at the entrance to Holkham Hall welcomes families. Refreshments are available at the Gift Shop and Pottery when the Hall is open.

Start

On the A149 coast road between Burnham Overy Staithe and Holkham. Half a mile east of Burnham Overy Staithe at the junction with the lane leading south to Burnham Thorpe. There is parking space here on both verges by the start of the footpath. Alternatively you could park along Lady Ann's Drive (there is a fee at weekends and in high season) and begin the walk from there, heading anti-clockwise perhaps in high easterly winds. O.S. TF 853 439 (Explorer Map 251).

Route

1. Take the footpath that forms the northerly arm of a crossroads with the A149 and the Burnham Thorpe road and head out towards the sea. Cross the stile and keep heading towards the dunes in a straight line, through a metal gate and up on to the sea wall. Turn right and continue along the sea wall on to a boardwalk. Where the boardwalk divides, go left and cross the dunes on to the beach.
2. Walk in an easterly direction, either along the beach or the dunes, for about 2 miles.
3. When you reach the wide sweep of Holkham Bay, turn inland, heading towards the rails that lead off the beach at the apex of the bay. Follow the boardwalk through the woods on to Lady Ann's Drive. Head southwards down the drive to the main road.
4. Cross the A149 and enter the drive of Holkham Hall immediately ahead of you. Pass through the entrance gates and keep heading straight on along the main drive. At the T-junction of the drive turn right to pass across the northern front of the Hall and down towards the lake.
5. Walk beside the lake around the west end of the Hall and then bear right around the end of the lake. Cross the cattle grid and continue straight on, passing the entrance to the nursery, and leave the park through the gates by the West Lodge.
6. Head straight along the lane that takes you on to the B1155. Turn left and walk along this road for ¾ mile (take care, especially at busy periods). At the next crossroads turn right on to a quieter lane which after another ½ mile will return you to the A149 and the start of the walk.

Summary

This is a town walk and almost entirely along paved streets but it includes a section through The Walks, a large open park of grass and tree-lined avenues. While the Old Town is well preserved with delightful lanes of ancient buildings, several areas of King's Lynn seem to have been decimated by road building. As far as possible, this walk takes you through the quieter streets but there is unavoidably a stretch of heavy traffic and some busy roads to negotiate.

Attractions

Still an active port today, King's Lynn was once one of the foremost ports in England and its prosperous maritime history is evident from every prospect of the Old Town. Those with a serious interest in Lynn's fascinating past should visit the famous Custom House on Purfleet Quay (a short detour at the start of the walk). Built in 1683 as a merchants' exchange, it now houses the Tourist Information Centre, selling guides and books as well as providing details of opening times of the various museums in the town.

King's Lynn boasts a wealth of fine buildings, but the most remarkable, after the Custom House, must be the Guildhall of the Holy Trinity, rebuilt after a fire in 1421 and housing the Town Hall and the Regalia Rooms, whose artefacts include the priceless 14th century King John's Cup. Trinity Guildhall and the 12th century St Margaret's Church together grace the most delightful corner of King's Lynn: the Saturday Market Place is said to display some of the finest ancient architecture in England. Its counterpart at the northern end of town – the Tuesday Market Place – impresses on a grander scale. It houses a thriving modern market and also hosts the Lynn Mart, a centuries old fair taking place on St Valentine's Day.

From the splendid open space of the Tuesday Market, you return to the starting point of the walk, via Lynn's two grandest thoroughfares – King Street and Queen Street, both lined with fine merchants' houses. Behind the restored timber shop fronts of 28–32 King Street lies the oldest secular building in the town of which the 12th century arcaded gable walls remain. Also on King Street is St George's Guildhall, the largest 15th century guildhall remaining in Britain. Since its creation in 1410, it has served as a warehouse, theatre, court house and armoury and is now home to the King's Lynn Centre for the Arts.

Respite from the cobbles and pavements of the Old Town can be found on the tree-lined avenue of The Walks. In the centre of the park stands the curiously shaped Red Mount Chapel. This strange squat tower was built about 1485 to accommodate pilgrims on their way to the holy town of Walsingham, explored in Walk 14.

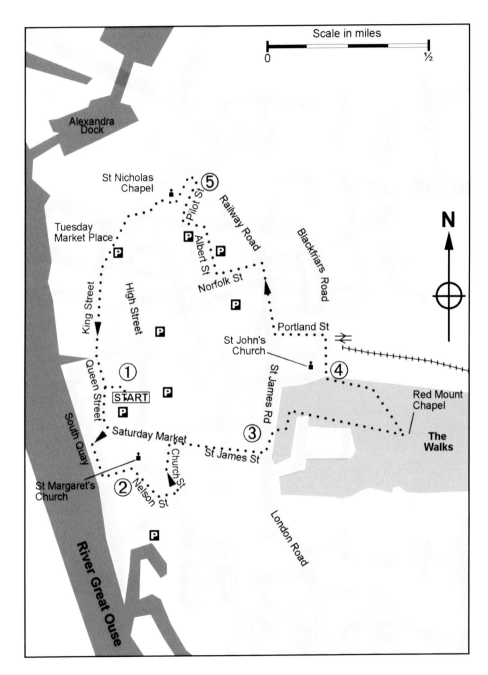

Scale in miles

0   ½

Alexandra Dock

St Nicholas Chapel

⑤

Pilot St

Railway Road

N

Tuesday Market Place

P

Albert St

P

Blackfriars Road

Norfolk St

P

King Street

High Street

P

Portland St

St John's Church

④

Queen Street

①

START

P

St James Rd

P

Red Mount Chapel

South Quay

Saturday Market

③

The Walks

St James St

St Margaret's Church

②

Church St

Nelson St

P

London Road

River Great Ouse

Refreshments

There is a huge choice of places to eat and drink in the town. For historic ambience, the Guildhall of St George on King Street has a coffee shop in the undercroft. Red Mount Chapel is situated in a large open park known as The Walks which is a good spot for a picnic.

Start

In the centre of King's Lynn at the Baker Street car park which is situated between Queen Street and the High Street, just north of the Saturday Market. There are a number of other car parks within very easy reach of this point and the bus and railway stations are a 5- and 10-minute walk respectively (see map). O.S. TF 616 199 (Explorer Map 236).

Route

1. From Baker Lane car park head away from the High Street towards the river, crossing over Queen Street and taking King's Staithe Lane. Turn left and walk along the South Quay alongside the Great Ouse. Take the next turning left down College Lane by the Youth Hostel to emerge opposite the Trinity Guildhall at the end of the Saturday Market Place.
2. Turn right along Nelson Street with St Margaret's Church on your left. Cross the junction with Priory Street and continue along Nelson Lane. At the end of Nelson Lane turn left up Church Street and then right along St James Street. Continue straight on over Tower Street, passing Greyfriars Tower and Gardens on your right.
3. Cross over London Road and turn left to enter the gate into the park (The Walks). Head to the fountain and from there strike out to your right across the grass to the Red Mount Chapel. At the Chapel turn left along a wide path and then left again at the tennis courts to follow the cycle/walkway to the road.
4. Turn right opposite St John's Church and head up Blackfriars Road past the railway station and then turn left along Portland Street. At the end turn right along Railway Road, cross the road, turn left down Norfolk Street and then right along Albert Street. At the end turn left and then right into Pilot Street.
5. Walk to the end of Pilot Street and then turn and retrace your steps to enter the churchyard of St Nicholas's Chapel, cutting the corner to emerge in St Ann's Street. Go straight on into St Nicholas Street which will lead you into the Tuesday Market Place. Circumnavigate the market place, leaving it ultimately at the south west corner along King Street which leads into Queen Street and then returns you to the starting point of the walk.

Summary

Apart from a stretch of 50 yards along a quiet lane, this walk is entirely on footpaths across some of the loveliest and most peaceful countryside in Norfolk. The water meadows and woods are rich in wildlife, and Itteringham, where the walk begins and ends, is a small but pretty village on the River Bure. There are good views of Mannington Hall, the gothic-style family seat of the Walpoles. The gardens (not the Hall) are open to the public on a regular basis and half-a-mile's detour from the route would take you to the entrance. Telephone 01263 584175 for opening times. At present careful walkers are positively welcomed on the Mannington estate and other land included in this walk but bear in mind that many of the numerous footpaths are of the permissive variety and should be used with special consideration. The landowners may alter routes from time to time and the paths through Mossymere Wood and the water meadows at the beginning of the walk are difficult to map and subject to natural change: to avoid confusion you should take an up-to-date OS map and maybe a compass on this walk.

Attractions

At the time of writing, much of the land on which this walk takes place is part of the Mannington estate and in the ownership of Lord Walpole – an enlightened peer with an interest in ecology and a genuine commitment to conservation. Since inheriting the property in 1989 he has attempted to show that

'farming, conservation and public enjoyment of the countryside can all combine to help preserve the special character of the countryside'.

The result is a pastoral haven and far removed from the intensively farmed acres that form the popular image of East Anglia. New trees have been planted and hedgerows maintained to provide habitats for wild grasses and herbaceous plants as well as birds and insects.

Water meadows, like those at the start and end of the walk, are increasingly rare as land is drained for agricultural use. In early summer yellow flag irises abound; look out for wild orchids as well – especially Common Spotted. You may see dragonflies, toads, water voles or, if you are lucky and out towards dusk, maybe even a barn owl.

From Duffer's Plantation you will have a good view of Mannington Hall, dating in part from 1461 and bought in the 18th century by Horatio Walpole, the brother of Sir Robert Walpole, England's first Prime Minister. You can also see the magnificent barn of Hall Farm, dating from the 1790s and now providing roosts for swallows, house martins and barn owls. The name 'Duffers' derives from dovehouse – there used to be one on this spot when pigeons were a significant part of the diet.

Mossymere Wood is the oldest woodland on the estate, half of it being classed as 'semi-natural ancient woodland' that has existed here for many hundreds of years. Most of the oaks would have been planted specifically for timber but other trees have seeded and grown naturally. In the dense shade beneath the beeches there is little

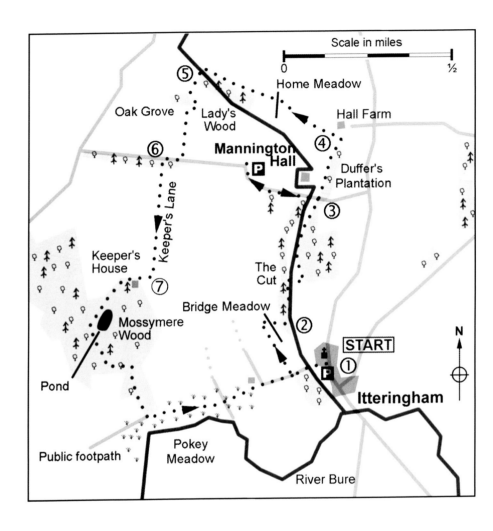

Scale in miles

0   ½

Home Meadow

Oak Grove   Lady's   Hall Farm
             Wood

⑤

⑥   Mannington   ④
     Hall   Duffer's
     P   Plantation

Keeper's Lane   ③

Keeper's   The
House   ⑦   Cut

Bridge Meadow

Mossymere   ②
Wood
                    START
Pond   ①

                    Itteringham

Public footpath   Pokey
                   Meadow

                   River Bure

N

plant life but where the leaf canopy is more open you will find many bluebells and primroses in Spring – so-called indicator species that tell us this is ancient woodland. Where there is bramble and honeysuckle in the more open spaces there are White Admiral butterflies.

Parts of the wood may seem untidy where fallen trees and log piles are left to rot but these provide perfect habitats for green woodpeckers and other hole-nesting birds as well as for a huge variety of bugs and beetles.

Refreshments

The Walpole Arms in Itteringham is a delightful pub serving good food. It has a large garden and welcomes families. Teas are available at Mannington Hall when the gardens are open (the entrance is a half-mile detour from the route of the walk).

Start

In the village of Itteringham 3 miles north-west of Aylsham. Park in the car park by the community centre which is just south of the church on the road that heads out of the village towards Matlaske. O.S. TG 145 309 (Explorer Map 252).

Route

1. Take the main track by the side of the community centre out of the car park (to your left as you look towards the church). Cross over the stream and after 200 yards (from the start) take a right turn over a stile (this should be opposite a footpath sign on your left). Follow the footpath signs along the edge of the water meadow (Bridge Meadow) and when the path forks take the path to your right. Follow the footpath signs along the meadow edge and at the corner of the meadow follow the path round to your right rather than turning left over the stile. After 50 yards cross a stile, a bridge and a second stile to bring you to a small wood known as 'The Cut'. (Avoid the very boggy – and probably overgrown – path halfway down Bridge Meadow that also crosses the stream into The Cut.)

2. Turn left to take the path that runs along the edge of the wood. Continue straight on, skirting a small glade and where the path forks turn right over a bridge. Cross over the stile into the meadow. Walk straight across the meadow and then turn left to walk along the edge of the field beside another wood until you reach a stile which takes you on to the road.

3. If you wish to visit the gardens or tea room at Mannington Hall turn left here and a short walk (¹⁄₄ mile) will bring you to the main gates. (You can also enter the gardens from a slightly later point.) Otherwise cross the road and the stile immediately opposite you and walk alongside Duffer's Plantation with fine views to your left of Mannington Hall. Walk straight up the edge of the meadow until you reach the end of the wood.

4. At the corner of the field and the wood, just before Hall Farm, turn left and head

along the field edge down towards a stile and a five-bar gate. Follow the path across the field to a second five-bar gate and stile. Cross the stile and continue straight on along the 'green lane' to a third stile (and gate), cross it and then cross the stream, bear slightly to your left and cross another stream to reach a fourth stile. Cross the stile and follow the path alongside Lady's Wood. You can enter the gardens of Mannington Hall by turning left at the end of the green lane before Lady's Wood and crossing the boardwalk over Home Meadow.

5. Just beyond the wood turn left and follow the edge of the field to your left around the end of the wood. At the corner of the field turn left through a gap into the adjoining field and then immediately right towards a small pine wood (called Oak Grove!), keeping the hedge on your right. Skirt the wood clockwise, turning right at the corner, and halfway along the southern side turn left away from the wood along the edge of the field keeping the hedge on your right.

6. When you reach the road turn right and walk for 50 yards. (If you wish to avoid walking on the road, there is a permissive path that runs alongside it through the strip of trees on your left but it can be difficult to access from the road.) Take a left turn down a track known as Keeper's Lane and marked 'Private Road. Estate Vehicles Only'.

7. At the bottom of the hill where the track divides follow it round to the right. With Keeper's House on your left follow a grassy track through a pedestrian gate beside a five-bar gate and continue to follow the track along the edge of the wood. Go down a hill and the path will emerge into a large glade, full of bluebells in the spring. Keep straight on into the heart of Mossymere Wood. After 50 yards bear left at the next fork and then follow the path as it bears round to your right around a large overgrown pond (maybe the original mossy mere?). At the T-junction of the path turn left down the hill into the open glade passing a large tree stump on your right. Turn right across the glade into the trees and then when the path forks follow it to the left through some swampy terrain; there should be two little bridges but one is very dilapidated (look out for sticklebacks in the stream). At the large ash tree on the corner bear right and then left to continue in the same line along the narrow over-hung path inside the edge of the wood. Keep following this path as it emerges into a scrubby wetland known as Pokey Meadow. Cross over a new metalled track, go over the stile and take the wooded path past a collection of derelict farm buildings. When you meet the next track bear slightly to your right through the gates and up the hill to return to the start of your walk.

Summary

This is an easy ramble on paths and tracks across Weybourne Heath and the landscaped grounds of Sheringham Park. An optional detour and a little extra effort will take you to the top of the gazebo from where there are wonderful views to the sea. You could combine the walk with a trip on the North Norfolk Railway or just watch the world – and the steam trains – go by from the station platform.

Attractions

The best way to arrive at the start of this walk is undoubtedly by steam train. The North Norfolk Railway (also known as The Poppy Line) runs trains regularly from the traditional seaside resort of Sheringham and from Holt, a Georgian market town linked to the station by horse-drawn bus. Tel. 01263 822045 for train times and fares. However you arrive, enjoy a moment of nostalgia in the charming little station.

The great landscape garden of Sheringham Park was declared by its designer, Humphrey Repton, himself to be 'my most favourite work'. Even before Repton refined and improved it, this was a lovely undulating landscape with superb natural vistas down to the cliffs and sea at Sheringham. Abbot Upcher, who bought the estate in 1811, declared

'What infinite variety presents itself in this enchanting spot... Oh! What scenes of rational yet heartfelt pleasure do we not anticipate in the lovely Sheringham.'

When Repton was commissioned by Upcher to remodel the estate he was at the height of his reputation although crippled by an accident in 1811. He knew Sheringham of old, having lived at nearby Sustead, and took on the project with great enthusiasm, outlining his plans for the park in one of his famous 'Red Books'. These red leather bound volumes allowed his clients to see 'before and after' versions of the same scene and were reserved for his most important works.

Sheringham Hall itself was designed by Repton's architect son John, but it was Humphrey who was responsible for the striking manner in which the house appears in the landscape, planned in a conscious fashion as was every view of sea and woodland. It is situated at a point in the main drive known as 'The Turn' where it

'will burst at once on the sight like some enchanted palace of a fairy tale'.

If you have a choice, come to Sheringham in May or June for its 50 acres of rhododendrons and azaleas. The planting probably began around 1850 with one of the tallest varieties, the red *Rhododendron arboreum*, and the purple *Rhododendron ponticum*. The latter quickly became invasive but has been brought under control in recent years. Up to 65 different species have now been added, many obtained early this century from the famous plant collector Ernest 'Chinese' Wilson, along with maple, pieris and magnolia. If you have a head for heights do climb the viewing towers which enable you to look down upon a sea of vibrant colour when the rhododendrons are in flower. A more strenuous climb will take you to the top of the gazebo for outstanding views of park and sea. It stands on the site of a look-out post erected during the Napoleonic wars.

57

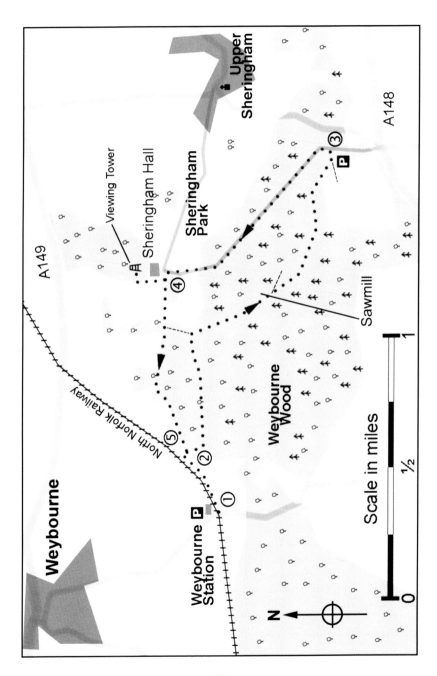

Weybourne

Upper Sheringham

Viewing Tower

Sheringham Hall

Sheringham Park

A149

A148

North Norfolk Railway

Sawmill

Weybourne Wood

Weybourne Station

Scale in miles

0   ½   1

N

Refreshments

There is a kiosk at the main entrance of Sheringham Park serving drinks and snacks every day during the summer and at most weekends. Weybourne Station has a café which again is open regularly during the high season. To dine as you travel, on the East Coast Pullman Restaurant, phone 01263 822045. Sheringham and Holt both offer a wide choice of cafés and pubs.

Start

At Weybourne Station, ½ mile south of Weybourne village. Approaching Weybourne from Sheringham on the A149 coast road, turn left opposite the church, following signs for the North Norfolk Railway. You may park in the station car park but if you are not catching a train the Railway would appreciate a donation. Or arrive by train from Sheringham or Holt. O.S. TG 117 419 (Explorer Map 252).

Route

1. If necessary, cross the footbridge so that you are on the south side of the track, go through the gate immediately under the bridge and turn left to follow the path alongside the railway line and then up a slight hill away from the track towards the pine wood.
2. When you reach the wood turn right along the track and then take the next left-hand fork. Keep straight on along the main track, ignoring a left-hand turn. About ½ mile into the woods, and at the junction of the main tracks, turn left, and at the next T-junction, turn right. Keep straight on, ignoring a turn to your right, and after 50 yards turn left down the track. At the next T-junction turn right and at the next fork (by the saw mill) bear right again. Take the next left-hand fork up the hill and then keep straight on down the hill, turn left at the T-junction and then right at the next junction to emerge into the car park. Refreshments are available here at the kiosk.
3. Follow the signs for the orange and blue waymarked walks out of the car park along the boardwalk. Turn left at the metalled drive and continue down this avenue of rhododendrons until you have crossed a cattle grid and are facing Sheringham Hall. (Look out for two left-hand turns along the drive to the viewing towers.)
4. With Sheringham Hall before you, turn left, following the sign to the Gazebo, and go through the gate. Here, if you wish, you can turn right, walk 100 yards and make the steep climb to the Gazebo, retracing your steps to continue the walk. From the gate, go straight on, following the sign to Weybourne Station along the edge of the field. Enter the wood and cross the barrier into Weybourne Heath. At the edge of the wood, continue straight on, following the track to the pine wood and then skirting its northern side, until you return to the point you had reached at number 2.
5. Turn right down the hill and follow the path along the railway to return to the station.

Summary

This is a long walk but it is all easy going, mainly on footpaths and lanes inland and along the sea wall at the beginning and end. It takes in five of the seven 'Burnhams', originally prosperous villages less than a mile apart. By adding on Walk 3 (Burnham Thorpe) and making a minor detour in Burnham Market you would be missing only Burnham Deepdale, a further half a mile to the west. This is a walk of contrast: between the peace and the beauty of the saltmarsh around Overy Creek and the bustling fashionable Burnham Market.

Attractions

The seven 'Burnhams' were once all prosperous villages and collectively a significant seaport. Today, Burnham Market dominates the local scene, absorbing the parishes of Burnhams Sutton, Ulph and Westgate. This little market town has one of the most attractive high streets in Norfolk and many fine Georgian houses. It is correspondingly fashionable and, boasting as it does a number of restaurants and delicatessens, makes a good place to break the walk. Two inns remind us that Admiral Nelson was born two miles south at Burnham Thorpe: the Lord Nelson and The Hoste Arms, named after a protégé of Nelson, later a great naval commander in his own right. The churches of Westgate and Ulph are at either end of the main street, while the ruins of St Ethelbert, Burnham Sutton, are situated on the Creake road.

This walk begins and ends at Burnham Overy, consisting of the 'Town' and the 'Staithe'. Burnham Overy Town – now a bit of a misnomer for a tiny hamlet – was once a small but thriving port serving the Creakes and the Burnhams. As the tides deposited sand and shingle from Yorkshire along the East Anglian coast, the sea receded and it became harder to navigate the River Burn into Overy Town, until at the end of the Middle Ages, the Staithe, or loading wharf, was established for the traffic of schooners and barges. Nelson is said to have first set sail from Overy Staithe, and Captain Woodget, Master of the *Cutty Sark*, made his home here. The port began to decline from 1866 with the coming of the railway to the Burnhams, with the last trading vessels calling here at the end of the First World War. Today it is a popular harbour for small yacht sailing.

The name 'Overy' probably derives from the Anglo Saxon *Offer*, meaning a river bank, which would be apt for such a watery place. There are two fine watermills here: one is situated on the coast road half a mile west of the Staithe, while you will pass the other as you walk between Burnham Market and Burnham Overy Town. Look to your left through a gap in the hedge just before you cross the mill stream for a view of St Mary's Friary. Burnham Overy Town is a picturesque cluster of cottages (with some impressive garden ornaments); the 13th century St Clements Church has an unusual central tower – strangely squat but apparently once higher. Of all the Burnham churches, St Margaret's at Norton is said to be the most interesting: the pulpit has a fine 15th century painting of Saints Ambrose, Augustine, Gregory and

61

Jerome, who were the founding theologians of the Western church, known collectively as the 'Four Latin Doctors'.

The coastal sections of the walk take you over the saltmarshes where sea lavender and sea aster thrive in the tidal cycles, as does the local delicacy of samphire or 'poor man's asparagus'. In summer the air is alive with skylarks and swifts while redshank and lapwing wade at the water's edge. Large populations of Brent and pink-footed geese arrive in winter, many roosting on nearby Scolt Head Island.

Refreshments

A wide choice in Burnham Market, from deli to tea shop to renowned fish restaurant. For the Hoste Arms Hotel, turn left along the village street. There is also a pub in Burnham Overy Staithe.

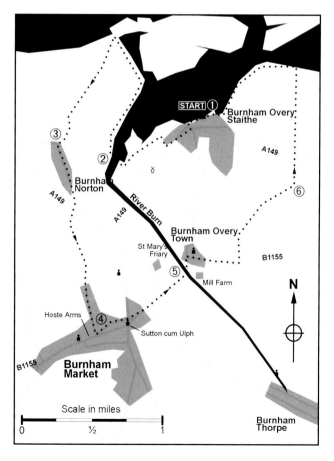

Start

Park on the harbour front at Burnham Overy Staithe on the A149 coast road west of Wells-next-the-Sea. O.S. TF 845 444 (Explorer Map 251).

Route

1. From the harbour at Burnham Overy Staithe head west and up on to the main road, then turn right and walk along the pavement to the end of the houses. After the last house turn right through a gap in the hedge and follow the path along the inside of the hedge. After 100 yards branch diagonally right across the field, following the footpath sign and heading towards a collection of farm buildings (the path may be cut through the crops). Cross the stile and continue straight on along the sea wall.

2. At the signpost on the corner follow the sea wall round to your right. (If you wish to take a short cut here, head straight on into the village of Burnham Norton. Rejoin the route at point 3.) At the next sharp left-hand bend, go down from the sea wall and follow the path by the five-bar gate to your left, heading back towards the village. Cross over the little wooden footbridge and the stile and continue on the track towards the village. Pass through an impressive series of gates and bear right at the footpath sign.

3. Pass in front of the cottages and turn left at the lane. Cross over the A149 coast road and head inland down the footpath immediately opposite. Follow the footpath along the left-hand side of the hedge to reach the next lane. Bear right here to bring you into Burnham Market.

4. Turn left along the village street and when you are ready, leave the village along Front Street and pass the church of Sutton cum Ulph. Bear left at the road junction and right at the next one (at the apex of the churchyard) to follow the B1155 road towards Cromer and Wells. (When the pavement on the left runs out cross the road and use the pavement on the right.) Look through a gap in the hedge on your left for a view of St Mary's Friary. Pass Mill Farm on your right, cross the mill stream and bear left. Cross the road again for safety just before following the road round the next right-hand bend.

5. This tiny hamlet is actually Burnham Overy Town. Continue eastwards with care along the B1155, pausing to visit the church on your left if you wish. Beyond the next group of houses (about $1/3$ mile) take the footpath to your left along the cinder track and then where the paths diverge head diagonally across the field to your right. The track should be cut clearly through any crops. Keep crossing a number of fields until you meet the road.

6. At the road turn left and after $1/4$ mile cross straight over the A149 coast road and follow the footpath out towards the dunes. Cross the stile into the nature reserve, pass through two gates and then up on to the sea wall. Turn left and head westwards along the sea wall to return to Burnham Overy Staithe.

Summary

The first part of this walk takes you through the ancient streets of Little Walsingham, an extraordinary village which has been a place of pilgrimage since medieval times. The route then leads along a quiet country lane to the Slipper Chapel and Roman Catholic shrine in the village of Houghton St Giles before returning via the historic Friday Market to the village high street. The walk can be extended by including the Abbey grounds, accessible every day during the summer months through the Shirehall Museum on payment of an entrance fee. Contact The Estate Office on 01328 820259 for opening hours.

The Wells and Walsingham Light Railway runs up to the coast from the outskirts of the village and, if you are feeling energetic, could enable you to take in Walk 15 on the same day! Phone 01328 710631 for details.

Attractions

Little Walsingham has been a place of pilgrimage since the 11th century when the Lady of the Manor, Richeldis de Faverches, had visions of the Virgin Mary and of the house in Nazareth where the Angel Gabriel had appeared to announce the birth of Christ. On the Virgin's command, Richeldis built a replica of the Holy House in Walsingham and the village became known as England's Nazareth. An Augustinian Priory and a Franciscan Friary were built in the 12th and 14th centuries and throughout medieval times pilgrims from all over Europe visited Walsingham and its shrine, among them most of the Kings and Queens of England. The last royal pilgrim was Henry VIII in 1511 – the last because he was later responsible for the dissolution of the monasteries, including Walsingham Priory and Friary in 1538.

For the next three centuries, Walsingham's renown was essentially as a market town and judicial centre, but towards the end of the 19th century a religious revival began which reached its climax in the 1930s with the establishment of the present Anglican and Roman Catholic shrines. Now, as in medieval times, Walsingham plays host to thousands of pilgrims every year and on feast days processions once more wend their way along the ancient paths between the holy sites.

The first of these that you will encounter is the Anglican Shrine containing the replica of the Holy House and the Holy Well dating back to Saxon times. Notice the small wooden door in the Priory wall opposite the entrance to the shrine. Known as the Knight's Gate, this was the legendary site of a miracle in 1314 when Sir Raaf Boutetout, fleeing his enemies, prayed to Our Lady for rescue and found himself and his horse transported through the original wicket gate into the Priory grounds and hence to sanctuary.

The High Street is a real-life lesson in the history of domestic architecture with fine timber-framed houses of the 15th and 16th centuries intermingled with 17th and 18th century facades. Martyr's House (now the Sue Ryder shop) is a particularly good example of a splendid Georgian facade on a much earlier building. (Members of the Walsingham Conspiracy – a plot against the closure of the monasteries – were

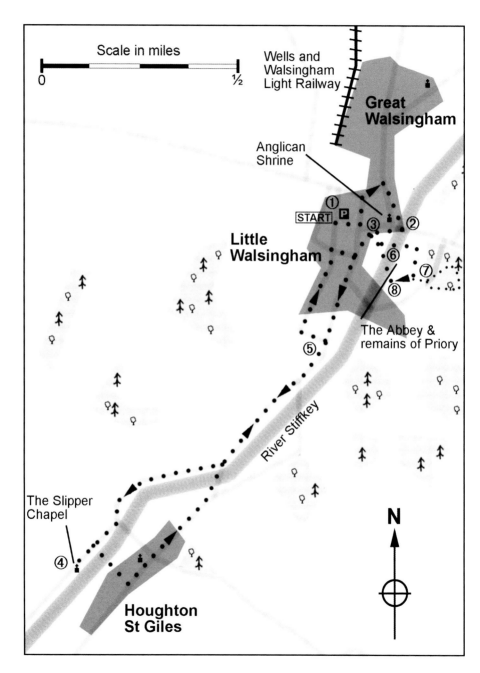

Scale in miles

0 ½

Wells and
Walsingham
Light Railway

Great
Walsingham

Anglican
Shrine

① START P

Little
Walsingham

③

② ②

⑥

⑦

⑧

The Abbey &
remains of Priory

⑤

River Stiffkey

The Slipper
Chapel

④

Houghton
St Giles

N

held prisoner here before being hanged, drawn and quartered at the nearby Martyr's Field.) Opposite the Martyr's House is the Gatehouse to the Priory: look up at the little window over the gateway to see the stone head representing both Christ and the porter.

The route out of the village to the Roman Catholic shrine is known as the Holy Mile and would have been walked barefoot by medieval pilgrims who would have removed their shoes at the last wayside chapel – the Slipper Chapel – built in 1325. Dedicated to St Catherine, the patron saint of pilgrims, the Chapel was dissolved in 1538 but its ruined remains were purchased during the Victorian religious revival and restored to allow the first Roman Catholic pilgrimage in 1897. It became the Roman Catholic National Shrine to Our Lady in 1934 and was later joined by the Chapel of Reconciliation, consecrated in 1982.

To extend this walk, or have a break from streets and roads, you can enter the Priory grounds. If you are in Walsingham in February, this really is a must for one of the best displays of snowdrops you could find. But the woods and meadow and the meandering River Stiffkey are delightful at all times of year. There are few remains of the original Priory buildings but the East Gable end of the Church is a striking survivor. Beyond this are the Holy Wells where, according to legend, Richeldis attempted to build the first Holy House, only for it to be miraculously moved overnight to firmer ground. The Packhorse Bridge, which is an excellent example of a medieval bridge, originally carried the main road to Norwich and lay outside the Priory Walls. The boundary was moved in the 19th century in order that the bridge could feature in the gardens.

Inevitably, it is only possible to touch on Walsingham's fascinating history in these pages. There are many books and guides available from local shops or the tourist office if you wish to learn more.

Refreshments

Plenty of choice of pubs and tea shops in Walsingham. Refreshments are also available at the Roman Catholic shrine.

Start

At Little Walsingham which is on the B1105 4 miles north of Fakenham. Park and start the walk in the car park just off the Common Place near the northern end of the High Street. O.S. TF 935 369 (Explorer Map 251).

Route

1. From the car park walk past The Bridewell or House of Correction (now a pine furniture warehouse) towards the Common Place and turn left along Bridewell Street. At the end of the street turn right along Guild Street opposite the Robin Hood Inn. After 100 yards turn right at the war memorial into Knight Street.
2. On the corner of Knight Street and the Holt Road you will find the Anglican Shrine

and opposite it The Knight's Gate. After visiting the Shrine turn right towards the village and enter the Common Place.

3. From here, if you wish to explore the Abbey grounds, you can enter through the Shirehall Museum in the Common Place. (A suggested route follows, numbers 6–8.) To continue the main route of the walk turn left down the High Street and carry straight on out of the village passing the ruins of The Friary on your right, heading southwards down the Holy Mile. After $\frac{1}{4}$ mile take the right-hand fork following signs to the Slipper Chapel and Shrine. Follow the course of the River Stiffkey for a further $\frac{1}{4}$ mile, then turn left, again signed to the Slipper Chapel.

4. To return to the village from the Slipper Chapel, take the first right-hand turn and cross over the ford. At the main road turn left, pass the church and continue straight across the crossroads. At the bottom of a small hill, just before a slight right-hand bend, take a footpath off to your left towards a white footbridge. Cross the bridge and turn right to retrace your steps back towards the village (turning left at the junction).

5. Just before the village turn left up a lane marked to the coach park and at the corner turn right into Back Lane to pass along the back of the Friary ruins. At the crossroads turn right (glance to your left to see the onion dome of the Russian Orthodox shrine) to take you into the Friday Market. Turn left and left into the High Street to return to your starting point.

Suggested route through Abbey grounds

6. Enter Abbey gardens through Shirehall Museum and turn left towards the ruins of the church. Pass through the imposing arch of the east gable end to explore the Well Garden and then turn left over the Packhorse Bridge. Walk up into the woods away from the river, passing through an old stone bridge underneath the road and a small wooden gate if you wish to explore the woods further.

7. Return via the gate and the tunnel beneath the bridge and start to retrace your steps towards the ruins, then bearing left at the fork and left again at a large beech. Continue straight on into the meadow and cross it, heading towards the church.

8. Cross the drive and follow signs to the River Walk, taking the path through the woods and across a footbridge over a weir. Continue skirting the inside of the wall until you return to the drive. Turn right along the drive and then left across the front of the house and left again alongside the ruins of the refectory. Turn right to head back to the Shirehall Museum.

Summary

This walk starts and ends at Wells-next-the-Sea with its working harbour and air of a traditional seaside resort. A mile's walk along 'The Bank' takes you to a superb beach where you have a choice between continuing along the sands or following the Norfolk Coast Path on the edge of the woods to Holkham Gap. You return to Wells via footpaths through Holkham Park. Only a few hundred yards at the end of the walk are along road, where there is a pavement. Note that Holkham Park is open all year round but gates close at 6.00 p.m. Entrance to the park is free but there is a fee to park on Lady Ann's Drive should you decide to start your walk from a different point.

Attractions

Do squeeze buckets and spades into your rucksack if you are doing this walk with small children: the beaches at Wells-next-the-Sea and Holkham – arguably two of the most beautiful in East Anglia – offer miles of fine sand backed by dunes and pines. But be warned if you intend to paddle: reaching the sea itself can mean a serious trek at low tide! At Wells the colourful beach huts on stilts create an atmosphere of New England while the breathtaking expanse of Holkham Bay made a bid for stardom during the closing credits of the 1998 Oscar-winning film *Shakespeare in Love*.

If you don't wish to walk along the beach or want some respite from the wind on a blustery day you can follow the course of both the Norfolk Coast Path and the Peddar's Way and walk parallel to the coast along the southern side of Wells Woods. These form part of a three-mile-long belt of woodland planted in the last quarter of the 19th century in order to reclaim agricultural land from windblown sand. The path here meanders gently through birch, broom and gorse along the edge of the pine woods which provide temporary shelter for large numbers of migrant birds in the autumn. Look out for pied flycatchers, redstarts, whinchats, pipits and even the very rare Pallas's warbler sighted some years on route from Siberia to South China.

The second half of the walk gives you the chance to sample a tiny corner of the vast estate of Holkham Hall – the Palladian home of the Earl of Leicester. This walk does not take in the Hall itself, which is included in Walk 9, but it would be easy to make a small detour to do so if you wished. The route does follow two glorious avenues of holm oaks as well as a path through peaceful woodland colourful with periwinkle, speedwell and campion in spring.

It is worth taking time to explore the little town of Wells before or after your walk. Its harbour is the only one in North Norfolk to retain a maritime trade, mainly small freighters carrying agricultural products, and fishing fleets, some supplying the whelk stalls along the quay. Although the waterfront has been carelessly developed over the years, Wells has not lost the character of an old sea port and behind the quay lies a network of picturesque 'lokes' or lanes running into The Buttlands – an open green created originally for archery practice and surrounded by fine Georgian houses. From the outskirts of Wells it is possible to take the narrow-gauge railway to Walsingham (see Walk 14).

Refreshments

Fish and chips and ice cream are plentiful in Wells and there are harbourside stalls selling local shellfish. A seaside café opens during the summer months at the beachward end of 'The Bank'. Teas are also available at the entrance to Holkham Hall and The Victoria Hotel has a garden and welcomes families.

Start

At the harbour car park in Wells-next-the-Sea. From the A149 (west) take the B1105 at the sharp right-hand bend just before you reach the town. If travelling from the east take the first turning into Wells from the A149 and follow signs to the harbour. The car park is at the westward end of the harbour. O.S. TF 914 437 (Explorer Map 251).

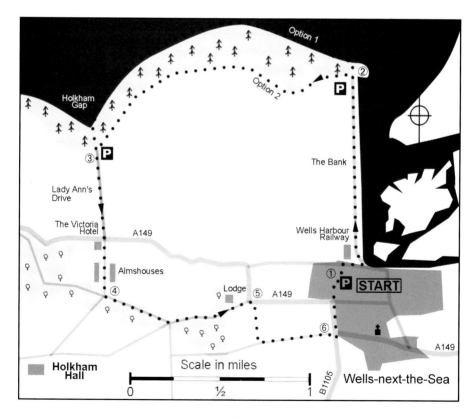

Route

1. From the car park walk down to Harbour Road and then turn right and head towards the quay. At the quay turn left to go over a bridge, then cross the road and take the path up on to the sea wall opposite The Harbour Station of Wells Harbour Railway. Head out to sea along 'The Bank'.

2. At the end of 'The Bank' you have a choice. Option 1 is to continue straight on past the Lifeboat Station on to the beach and then walk westwards along the sands for 1½ miles to Holkham Gap. Follow the boardwalk off the beach and through the woods to the seaward end of Lady Ann's Drive. Then continue the walk from Point 4 of the route.

2. Option 2 (advisable on very windy days) is to turn left near the end of 'The Bank' to head down to the beach café. Follow the road round the seaward end of the car park and then take the footpath through the gate and round the seaward end of the boating lake. Where the path divides take the left-hand fork and follow the course of the Norfolk Coast Path and Peddars Way. Where the path divides again turn right towards the woods and then continue to follow the long-distance footpath along the edge of the pine woods for 1½ miles until you reach Lady Ann's Drive. If you wish to take a look at Holkham Beach (and you should) turn right here and follow the boardwalk through the woods, later retracing your steps to continue the walk.

3. Walk southwards down Lady Ann's Drive, cross the main road (A149) and continue along the driveway towards Holkham Hall between Holkham Pottery and The Victoria Hotel. When you reach the main entrance gates (with cattle grid, by almshouses) note that all entrance gates to Holkham Park are closed at 6.00 p.m. Don't get locked in!

4. Pass through the gates and turn immediately left to follow a footpath through the wood. After 100 yards go through another gate and continue along the path which will bear round to the right just before coming to a five-way crossroads. Take the first left along a metalled track still within the wood. Go through the gate by the lodge and down an avenue of holm oaks.

5. When you reach the main road take a right turn just beyond the bend and follow a track which will curve first to the left around a farm building and then to the right across a field. Follow the track down the field to the bottom of the hill. Turn left along another track and continue until you reach the road.

6. At the road turn left through the remains of an old railway bridge. Cross the road to make use of the pavement. Cross the Cromer Road and continue straight on. Where the main road bends to the left continue heading straight on, following signs marked Beach and Car Park and then follow the road as it bends round to your right to take you back to the start of your walk. Any of the picturesque little lanes to your left will bring you out on the Harbour Road.

Summary

This is, in essence, a gentle stroll though there is a bit of a clamber down one hill and quite a steep – but short – climb up again towards the end. The walk is entirely on paths across heath and woodland, some of which may be very muddy during or after wet weather.

Attractions

This walk begins and ends at the highest point in Norfolk – a dizzying 100 metres. Although vertigo is unlikely to prove a problem, there are wonderful views along the coast, particularly of the rather aptly named Beeston Bump.

The area known as the Roman Camp derives its name from the ancient earth-works near the car park. There is no evidence that the Romans actually resided here but they almost certainly used the spot as a look-out, as would have many others throughout history, hence the point's alternative name of Beacon Hill. Further west, on Beeston Regis Heath, shallow pits can still be seen where local iron ore was smelted during the Middle Ages.

This ridge of little hills was formed 10,000 years ago from the debris of retreating glaciers, and its heathland covering created and maintained many thousands of years later by the clearing of woodland for sheep grazing. The woods and heath of Beeston Regis and the Roman Camp, along with Town Hill and Incleborough Hill to the east, are now all in the care of the National Trust who have worked to control bracken and encroaching trees and restore traditional heathland, colourful with heather in the summer months.

Within the woodland, oak, sweet chestnut and beech predominate though there are areas of dense silver birch and rowan, which began to invade the heathland when sheep grazing ceased.

A visit during a damp autumn should show you many varieties of fungus, while in spring and summer you may spot Gatekeeper or Holly Blue butterflies.

Refreshments

None actually available on the walk but there are shops and cafés in West Runton. Sheringham and Cromer offer a wide choice, even out of season.

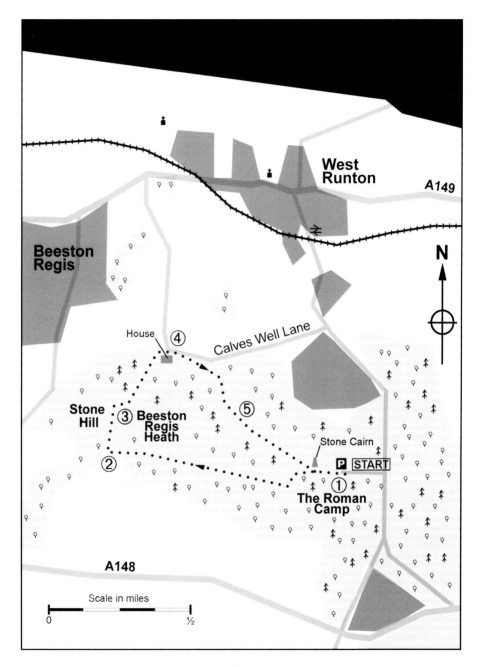

West
Runton

A149

N

Beeston
Regis

Calves Well Lane

House ④

⑤

Stone
Hill ③ Beeston
Regis
Heath

Stone Cairn

🅿 START

②

① The Roman
Camp

A148

Scale in miles
0   ½

Start

In the National Trust car park at the Roman Camp, 1 mile south of West Runton. Take the B road named Sandy Lane which links the A148 Holt–Cromer road and the A149 coast road. There is a small parking fee except for National Trust members. O.S. TG 184 414 (Explorer Map 252).

Route

1. From the car park take the track which runs from the end of the road alongside the caravan park and straight on into the woods. At the crossroads in the clearing turn left and then follow the main path round to the right and continue straight on along the main track.

2. After almost ¾ mile you will reach a kind of T-junction where you should bear right. At the corner of the boundary fence turn left along it and then take the first path to your right to bring you out on Beeston Regis Heath. Head for the highest point at Stone Hill where you will find a bench. Sit down and enjoy the view.

3. Head down the rather steep track immediately in front of the bench and at the bottom of the hill take a right turn along Calves Well Lane. When you meet the next track bear left, effectively to continue straight on. Pass a prettily situated house on your right and continue straight on again along the track.

4. At the crossroads and signpost go straight on, keeping the woods on your right, and at the next fork bear to your right through the barrier. Keep the wire fence on your right and follow the path as it curves round to the right into the wood. After 50 yards take a wide path off to your left up the hill and at the top of the hill turn right.

5. Cross the heath and then take a path to your right back into the woods. At the stone cairn turn left along the track to return to the car park.

Places to Visit

Nature Reserves and Nature Trails

Blakeney Point 01263 740480 (summer), 740241 (winter)
Cley Marshes Nature Reserve, Holt 01263 740008
Foxley Wood, Foxley   01362 688706
Natural Surroundings Wildflower and Countryside Centre, Holt 01263 711091
RSPB Reserve, Titchwell. Contact RSPB Norwich 01603 661662
Wolterton Park, Erpingham 01263 584175

Historic Buildings and Museums

Blickling Hall, Aylsham 01263 738030
Cromer Museum, East Cottages, Tucker Street, Cromer 01263 513543
EcoTech Discovery Centre, Swaffham 01760 726100
Felbrigg Hall, Cromer 01263 837444
The Green Quay Discovery Centre, King's Lynn 01553 818500
Holkham Hall and Bygones Museum, Wells-next-the-Sea 01328 710227
Houghton Hall, King's Lynn 01485 528569
Inspire Science Centre, Norwich 01603 612612
Letheringsett Watermill, Holt 01263 713153
Muckleburgh Collection Military Museum 01263 588608
Norfolk Rural Life Museum and Farm, Gressenhall, Dereham 01362 860563
Norwich Castle Museum 01603 493625
Sandringham House, King's Lynn 01553 772675
The Shell Museum, Glandford, Holt 01263 740081
The Thursford Collection, Fakenham 01328 878477
Walsingham Abbey Grounds and Shirehall Museum 01328 820259

Wildlife Collections

Banham Zoo 01953 887771
Norfolk Shire Horse Centre, West Runton 01263 837339
Norfolk Wildlife Park, Great Witchingham 01603 872274
The Otter Trust, Earsham 01986 893470
Pensthorpe Waterfowl Park and Nature Reserve, Fakenham 01328 851465
Sealife Aquarium, Hunstanton 01485 533576
Thrigby Hall Wildlife Gardens, Great Yarmouth 01493 369477

Country Parks and Gardens

Alby Crafts Gardens, Erpingham 01263 761590
Blickling Hall, Aylsham 01263 738030
Fairhaven Gardens Trust, South Walsham 01603 270449
Felbrigg Hall, Roughton, Cromer 01263 837444
Holkham Hall Gardens and Nursery, Wells-next-the-Sea 01328 711636

Holt Country Park 01263 516062/712610
Mannington Gardens and Countryside, Near Saxthorpe 01263 584175
Norfolk Lavender, Heacham, King's Lynn 01485 570384
Priory Maze and Gardens, Beeston Regis, Sheringham 01263 822986
Sandringham Grounds, King's Lynn 01553 772675
Sheringham Park, Upper Sheringham 01263 823778
Walsingham Abbey Grounds 01328 820259
West Acre Gardens, King's Lynn 01760 755562

Sports and Family Fun

Blakeney Point Sailing School, Glandford, Holt 01263 740704
Children's Indoor Adventure Funhouse, Wells-next-the-Sea 01328 711656
Dinosaur Adventure Park, Lenwade 01603 870245
Elephant Playbarn, Knapton 01263 721080
Fun Stop, Louden Road, Cromer 01263 514976
Sheringham Splash Leisure Complex, Sheringham 01263 825675
West Runton Riding Stables 01263 837339

Theatres

Norwich Puppet Theatre 01603 629921
Pavillion Theatre, The Pier, Cromer 01263 512495
Sheringham Little Theatre, Station Road, Sheringham 01263 822347

Railways

Bure Valley Railway, Aylsham to Wroxham 01263 733858
North Norfolk Railway, Sheringham to Holt 01263 822045
Wells and Walsingham Light Railway, Talking Timetable 01328 710631

Ancient Monuments

Castle Acre, Swaffham 01760 755394
Castle Rising, King's Lynn 01553 631330
Grimes Graves flint mines, Thetford 01842 810656
Norwich Castle 01603 493624/493625

Craft Centres

Alby Crafts, Erpingham 01263 761590
Caithness Crystal Visitor Centre (Glassmaking), King's Lynn 01553 765111
Great Walsingham Barns, Great Walsingham, Fakenham 01328 820900
Langham Glass, Near Blakeney 01328 830511
Wroxham Barns 01603 783762

Useful Information

Tourist Offices

Cromer: Bus Station, Prince of Wales Road 01263 512497
Fakenham: Oak Street 01328 850102
Holt: 3 Pound House, Market Place 01263 713100
Hunstanton : The Green, Greevegate 01485 532610
King's Lynn: The Custom House, Purfleet Quay 01553 763044
North Walsham: 32 Vicarage Street 01692 407509
Sheringham: Station Approach 01263 824329
Walsingham: Shire Hall Museum 01328 820510
Wells-next-the-Sea: Staithe Street 01328 710885

Organisations

Coastguard 0870 600 6505
English Heritage 020 7973 3434
English Nature 01603 620558
National Trust 01263 738000
Norfolk Naturalists Trust 01603 270337
Norfolk Wildlife Trust 01603 625540
North Norfolk District Council 01263 513811
Ramblers Association (Norfolk) 01603 612644
Royal Society for the Protection of Birds 01603 661662

Market Days

Aylsham: Monday (auction sales), Tuesday, Friday
Cromer: Friday
Fakenham: Thursday
Hunstanton: Wednesday, Sunday
King's Lynn: Tuesday, Friday, Saturday
North Walsham: Thursday
Sheringham: Saturday, Wednesday
Wells-next-the-Sea: Wednesday (Summer only)